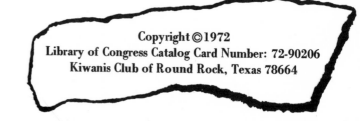

Round Rock, Texas, U. S. A. !!!

PROJECT OF ROUND ROCK KIWANIS CLUB

Martin E. Parker, President
Project Coordinator

Arnold Peterson
Photographer

Noel Grisham, Editor
Glyn Morsbach, Layout
Joan Baker, Publicity

Steering Committee:

Martin E. Parker
Robert G. Griffith
Mrs. J. W. Ledbetter
Mrs. Nancy Rabb
Arnold Peterson

Chairmanships:

Local Business—Rev. Gus Sager
Historical Pictures—Mrs. D. B. Gregg
Municipal Government—Cody Adolphson
Restored Homes—Mrs. Nathan Smith
Churches—Rev. Oliver Berglund
Schools—Claude T. Berkman
Memorials—Martin E. Parker

Clubs and Organizations—
 Rudolph Peterson and
 C. D. Fulkes
Youth Groups—Mr. & Mrs. Don Hester
Agriculture—Elmer Cottrell
Families—Xenia Voigt
Human Interest—Mrs. Robert L. Reed

1972

Sweet Publishing Co. and Henington Publishing Co.
Round Rock and Wolfe City, Texas

A PEOPLE WITH NO REVERENCE FOR THE HERITAGE LEFT THEM,
WILL INDEED LEAVE NOTHING OF THEMSELVES TO BE REMEMBERED PROUDLY***

With the above thought in mind, the Kiwanis Club of Round Rock decided to try and do something about the heritage left them. Round Rock is a very historical town with a very interesting heritage. It will be the desire and goal of this club, with the help of many interested citizens who are not Kiwanians, to publish this pictorial book so the present and future generations will have a record of history that came before them.

THE 1972 KIWANIS CLUB OF ROUND ROCK, TEXAS

Front Row: George Matthews; Glyn Morsbach, Secretary; Martin E. Parker, President; Virgil Rabb; Noel Grisham; Rudolph Pettersen; Charles Johnson.

Middle Row: Gus W. Sager; Michael Grimes; George Bujnoch; Stewart Dahlin; Freddie Bradley; Jack Hoover, Vice President; Carl Beard; Dwight Lamb; Ray Sanders; M. J. Cowan; Osie Crain, Treasurer; and W. Carroll Allen, Jr.

Back Row: Eugene Quick; Wayne Mann; Oliver Berglund; C. D. Fulkes; Bob Parker; Robert Griffith; W. G. McCoy; N. G. Whitlow; and D. Kent Berry.

Members not present for picture: Robert E. Johnson; Vonnie Tucker; Dennis Templeton; Earl Seay; Wayne King; Elwin Hudson; L. G. Cunningham; Nolen Balch; George Lovett; and Col. William N. Todd.

Spanish American soldiers parade down main street.

Uncertainty and obscurity prevent the fixing of an exact date for the beginning of Round Rock which was first called Brushy. As early as 1833 the area of Round Rock in Williamson County was providing opportunities for settlement by the white man. Tumlinson Fort was built west of Round Rock at the headwaters of Brushy Creek as an outpost for the protection of whites and friendly Indians of the area. The Comanche Indians were stern enemies of the Tonkawa, the friendly and more nearly civilized tribe which lived along the banks of the Brushy Creek (called by eighteenth century European explorers "Creek of the Blessed Souls"). Indian mounds and campsites are found in abundance from west of Round Rock to the Hutto area. Collectors of Indians relics continue to find, on surface and through mound diggings, many fine relics left by the redman.

Four years after Fort Tumlinson was established, another fort was established about two miles east of Round Rock on Brushy Creek south of the present Palm Valley Lutheran Church. This fort was built by Dr. Kenney, a medical doctor in the Texas Revolutionary Army. Dr. Kenney, together with a pioneer Round Rock settler, Capt. Nelson Merrell, carried on farming interests and capitalized on a good market for buffalo hides and mustang horses. Kenney's Fort, also called Fort Cazeneau, was the site of Texas' Archives War, the historic battle in which not one shot was fired. After this battle, the State Capitol was no longer in transit and was restored to Austin. Also, it was here that the Santa Fe pioneers were organized.

With the passing of Indian and Mexican opposition to white settlers the forts were no longer needed and Round Rock was soon to emerge as a significant early frontier town. Many Swedish families including the Nelsons, Jacksons, Gustafsons, Andersons, Johnsons, Berkmans, and Petersons came to Round Rock following S. M. Swenson and Swante Palm, fellow countrymen who had well established themselves in business and farming.

The town of Brushy came to be called Round Rock in the year 1854 when the first post office was established. Very soon there was to be Old Round Rock and New Round Rock with Brushy Creek as a boundary line between the two early settlements. With the coming of the railroad in 1876, the Texas Land Company aided in developing a new township at the end of the line. As the western-most limits of the railroad, Round Rock became a booming and prosperous trade center. Merchants came from San Antonio and Austin from the south and from settlements further west to pick up in wagons the merchandise and goods coming in by rail from the North and East.

The TEXAS NEW YORKER, in its February, 1878 issue, describes the towns of Central Texas. Round Rock had 1,500 people; Taylor had 250 settlers. Round Rock had fourteen general merchandise stores, four drug stores, four lumber yards, one bakery, six hotels and other shops. (At this date Austin had only five hotels compared to Round Rock's six.) The TEXAS NEW YORKER stated this about Round Rock in 1878: "The trade of Round Rock is very extensive, and includes a large portion of Williamson County, the Counties of Burnet, Lampasas, SanSaba, Mason, Llano, McCulloch, Concho, Coleman, Brown and portions of Comanche and Hamilton Counties. Round Rock is the actual gateway to ten of the finest and most rapidly growing frontier counties in Texas . . . ."

With Round Rock's strategic location, educational institutions were established between the time of the Civil War and the turn of the century. Greenwood Masonic Institute dates from the close of the Civil War. Soon after the establishment of this school, the Presbyterians established Round Rock Institute with a fine faculty of the sholars from the North and East. Classical studies were stressed. Latin and Greek were offered on a four year basis. Rev. C. H. Dobbs was the institutions' distinguished principal. The Lutherans established Trinity Junior College which continued until the early 1930's. With the closing of the junior college, there succeeded a children's home then a home for the aged on the old campus in the eastern part of New Round Rock.

In the year 1870, John Wesley Hardin, "Fastest Gun in the West" came to Round Rock and graduated from school with his brother Joe. At this time Professor Landrum, friend of the fast gun's Methodist Circuit-riding preacher father, administered a test to "Wes". As an able and "fast" student, Wes passed the test and graduated. Wes Hardin, then eighteen years old, and with eighteen notches on his gun, was being pressed by the Texas Rangers who had followed him from Brenham where he had been gambling and attending horse races with Bill Longley, "The Texan."

Since in early days almost all Central Texas roads led to prosperous Round Rock, another notorious bad man found his way to the thriving town at the intersection of the Chisholm Trail and Brushy Creek. But it was a one-way trip to Round Rock for "Texas Beloved Bandit" or "Robin Hood on a Fast Horse,"—Sam Bass. Sam's attempted bank robbery led only to the digging of new graves after the fury of gun battle on Main Street, Round Rock. Sheriff Grimes and Sam Bass went to their common and long home at the western limits of Old Round Rock while Frank Jackson, one of Bass' more fortunate accomplices, moved further west and, as legend suggests, became a respected medical doctor in Arizona.

Significantly, both the good and bad grow side by side, even in Round Rock. If it can be said that Round Rock attracts bad men, it also can be said that Round Rock produces good men as well. Ira Aten, protagonist of a new book by Hastings House Publishers—THE LONE STAR MAN, portrays the dignity and prowess of the Texas Ranger. Aten was reared in Round Rock. Like Wes Hardin, Aten was the son of a preacher, but similarity ended here. After a successful and colorful career as a Ranger, Aten retired to California and helped develop the Imperial Valley which honors him by giving his name to one of its prominent streets.

Round Rock in recent years has recaptured some of its earlier pioneer spirit and has restored some of its zest for enterprise and growth. Its educational system has been expanded and developed into one of the better systems of Central Texas. Banking and business in general is beginning to expand. Increase in the value of land is becoming phenomenal. Lime plants, stone quarries, burned dolomite processing plants, Texas Instruments, and Westinghouse, supply Round Rock with vigouous industry. Cattle and sheep raising together with farming keep the Round Rock economy stimulated.

Through the recent benevolence of Mr. and Mrs. Louis Henna, the Baptists of Texas have established Round Rock one of their largest children's homes. Trinity Lutheran Home, under the guidance of the Lutheran Welfare Society, is expanding into one of the State's finest homes for the aged.

The expanding, historic town, superbly located as a gateway to the State Capital and the Highland Lakes, keep pace with Texas progress. Historically rich in pleasure and pathos, and as a mecca for a large area with beautiful homes on oak-shaded acres, the emerging suburban city of Round Rock continues to display an exciting blend of the old and the new.

THE ROUND ROCK

FOR EARLY TRAVELERS, THIS UNUSUAL STONE MARKED SAFE, ROCK LINED FORD AT BRUSHY CREEK. 130 YEAR OLD WAGON RUTS SHOW HISTORIC ROADWAY. "BRUSHY" POST OFFICE WAS LOCATED NEAR FORD, 1851. AT WISH OF POSTMASTER T. C. OATS, IT WAS RENAMED "ROUND ROCK" IN 1854 AND RETAINED NAME WHEN TOWN MOVED EAST.

The above inscription is on the official Texas Historical Marker which was dedicated November 7, 1971. Mayor Dale Hester, Postmaster Martin E. Parker, School Superintendent, Noel Grisham, James D. Watson, Baptist minister, and Oliver Berglund, minister of Palm Valley Lutheran Church.

HISTORICAL

IT WILL BE THE INTENTION TO BRING YOU THE PROGRESS
OF ROUND ROCK BY STARTING IN "OLD TOWN" WHERE THE TOWN BEGAN
AND BUILDING AS NEAR AS POSSIBLE TO THE PRESENT'

MAIN STREET OF OLD TOWN
ROUND ROCK, TEXAS

This is a picture of the wooden bridge leading into "Old Town" around the turn of the century. This was also the Chisholm Trail used to drive herds of cattle to market. Sam Bass rode over this bridge mortally wounded after an attempted bank robbery and later taken over same bridge to be buried in the cemetery in Old Town.

The Round Rock for which the town is named is under this bridge. The house on the left is still partially standing and known as the Jessie Sansom home. The building on the right was the church. The two story home in the background was the Ledbetter home where Elmer Hester now lives. The store past the church was the Mays and Black store. The oak trees in the middle of the street are still growing in Old Town.

The bridge was dismantled during World War II and the metal supports used in the scrap metal drives.

This 1860 picture of the Alex Harris Store in "Old Town" is one of the oldest pictures available. It tells a story of how traders would come to town and barter for goods. Trading hides and farm produce was a way of life to get food.

This view of "Old Town", which at the time was the only town, was made prior to 1900. Picture was made from atop the first public school that was first used as the Southern Presbyterian Institute. The railroad bridge was washed out in 1900.

View of flood waters that washed out bridge in 1913. Ledbetter home in background.

View after water goes down.

Rebuilding and repairing the damage.

View looking west before 1900.

Low-water bridge used to get across brushy.

The top picture is the Smith Hotel and it was located in the 100 block of W. Bagdad St. where the W. J. Walsh home is now. With the coming of the railroad in 1876, the town site moved to where the town is now located. People had to have hotels to stay in since Round Rock was the "end of the line." The little girl on the steps is Mabel Hiddleson who is now 84 years old and pictured to the right. She was 14 yrs. when the picture was taken. She holds her little dog "Pug". The Smith Hotel was built in 1878.

The middle picture is of the Euhl Hotel and Mrs. J. D. Heath is standing in front of it.

*C*APITAL *M*EMORIAL *P*ARK, *I*NC.

RT. 2, BOX 76 ROUND ROCK. TEXAS 78664

9

RAILROADING IN AND THROUGH ROUND ROCK

In 1876-78, a railroad was built across the southern part of Williamson County by the International & Great Northern Railway Company. The track crossed Brushy Creek about two miles below the town of Round Rock, then located on the north side of Brushy, and terminated in 1876 just short of the proposed Lake Creek bridge site, where a depot and a freight station were built.

A new business community was quickly built at the temporary railhead, including several hotels, freight warehouses and other service stores. The new town assumed the name of Round Rock, and the town north of Brushy became known as "Old Town".

For the following decade, Round Rock prospered as the freight terminal and trading center for the area to the northwest as far as San Saba.

In 1878, the Georgetown Railroad Company built a railroad, tapping the I&GN main line at Round Rock. The road, called "The Tap", crossed Brushy Creek just above the round rock and terminated on the bank of the San Gabriel River in Georgetown. No turn-around facilities were built into the trackage, so the locomotive was equipped with a head lamp and a wooden pilot, or "cow catcher", both on the front of the engine and on the rear of the tender. The locomotive went forward pulling the train to Georgetown, then backing past the train on a siding, coupled the front end of the engine to the southbound train and backed back into Round Rock.

THIS PAGE COMPLIMENTS OF TEXAS CRUSHED STONE COMPANY
GEORGETOWN, TEXAS

The top pictures on both pages shows the locomotive, a 4-4-0 coal burner, built in the late 1880's, and equipped with then modern acetylene burning headlamps. The top picture on left was made in 1904 in present day Round Rock and preparing to make the trip to Georgetown. Picture of the train above is "Backin'-in" from Georgetown. Train carried both freight and passengers. The family having a picnic on the rocky banks of Brushy Creek in Old Town, is the W. J. Walsh family, in 1904. The train engineer was Jim Doughty, Fireman was Mr. Shadd, Ticket Agent, Mr. Mimms and the brakeman, John Hall.

The picture at the bottom of the opposite page was taken in 1922 and shows a 2-8-2 oil-burning light "Mike" as it pulls a north bound train from Austin through Round Rock. This locomotive is a Mikado type, the first of which was built for the Japanese National Railroad in 1895.

The Georgetown Railroad Company's financial structure collapsed and the I&GN purchased the trackage at receiver's sale in 1879. "The Tap" was consolidated with the I&GN in 1882. In 1956, the I&GN became a part of the Missouri Pacific. The present Georgetown Railroad Company, Inc., of which Mr. W. P. Ludwig is president, is sponsoring this page.

January 10, 1900 picture of the railroad bridge in "Old Town". Old grist mill on left.

THIS PAGE COMPLIMENTS OF GEORGETOWN RAILROAD COMPANY

The David William "Dude" Anderson family standing in front of home built in 1849. Picture made in 1898. "Dude" Anderson standing far right. His mother and dad standing and grandmother sitting. House still standing west of Round Rock.

This blacksmith and wheelright shop was located in the 100 Block of Lampasas St. where Theo Zimmerman's shop is now. This was a necessary business in the year 1880 when this picture was made.

Above: Robert Egger, Ida Canoval, Nettie Bradley, Elizabeth Landrum. Standing: Cecil Thorpe, Jewell Cluck, Floy Wright, LaNella Chambers. Kneeling: Louis Aten, Ivan Aten and Cecil Cochran, On the Round Rock! On right: Country Hog Killing with J. N. Wright, Roy Wright and Leon Wright on Weber Farm in Merrelltown.

COMPLIMENTS OF MRS. J. R. WRIGHT, LAS CRUCES, NEW MEXICO

Round Rock Creamery in 1904. Located on Brushy Creek where the Bennie Bustin home is now located. Farmers brought milk, it was separated and the farmers returned home with their skimmed milk. The business failed due to the lack of refrigeration. Archie Hester buggy on left, Simon Burkland in middle and Carl A. Anderson on right. Rueben Jacobson standing by buggy wheel on left. F. L. Aten was plant manager.

COMPLIMENTS OF FRED M. AND ESTER ANDERSON, 204 N. STONE.

The Public Well and Cover that furnished water for citizens prior to 1900 was also used as a community gathering place. The replica that is now standing, was built in 1970 by Bennie Bustin and Jimmie Yanero and Martin Parker did the rock work around the well.

An undated picture of Round Rock looking north from where the overpass is now built. Believed to be quite awhile before the turn of the century. Old post office building in foreground and Dr. Harrell's office across the street. Post office building was built in 1878.

The Old Cotton Yard in "The Flat" in 1900 with some 8,000 bales of cotton, J. M. (Mack) Jester, Merrell Jester, Johnnie Jester and Charlie Cockran. Picture facing east with house in background at 106 E. Anderson

COMPLIMENTS OF TAYLOR BEDDING COMPANY—SINCE 1903—MORNING GLORY PRODUCTS

The Alcove—Popular Ice Cream Parlor during the late 20's and early 30's on Main St. L. to R.: Lee McDonald, Bob Carlson, Ansel Nelson, Morris Ledbetter and J. W. Ledbetter.

COMPLIMENTS OF FRITO-LAY, INC.

THE BROOM FACTORY BUILDING was erected in 1876. Factory moved from old town into this building in 1887 and operated until 1912. A broom made in this building was entered in the 1904 World's Fair in St. Louis, Mo. and won a gold medal. The building is now a recorded Texas Historical Landmark. Present owner is Mr. Roger Burleson.

Working crew of the broom factory. This was the largest broom factory in Texas. L. to R.: Bob Crimm, Posey Awalt, Ed Anderson and the rest unknown.

"Baby" Harvey in 1912 at the recreation area at the dam in Old Town. Area had bath-house, refreshments and was lighted with electric lights. At right, is "Uncle" Clem Harvey, Deliveryman for W. J. Walsh Store.

Above—W. J. Walsh family in front of Trinity College in 1907. Below—Will C. Walsh with drums. 4 years old.

Early winter street scene in 1922

Snowed in railroad depot. 1922

17

TRINITY LUTHERAN COLLEGE

FOUNDED BY THE Augustana Lutheran Synod, in 1904 Synod representatives, seeking a location, selected Round Rock because of an offer of a well, 14 city lots and freight concessions on building materials hauled by International & Great Northern Railroad, Mr. J. A. Nelson gave the lots, the well and made arrangements with the I. & G. N. Railroad for the purchase of three acres additional land for $50.00 per acre which brought the campus to a 10 acre site. Corner-stone was laid July 13, 1905.

With Dr. J. A. Stamline serving as president, first session opened October 2, 1906. There were four faculty members, 48 academic students, and 11 enrolled in the music department. Total enrollment rose to 96 during the first year. Successive presidents were Alfred Anderson, 1909-1914; Theodore Seashore, 1914-1921; Dr. J. A. Stamline and Oscar Nelson, Adinterim, 1921-1923; and Harry A. Alden, 1923-1929.

Despite such recognition as state accreditation (achieved in 1920) school failed financially. In 1929 it merged with Evangelical Lutheran College which was founded in 1891 at Brenham, moved to Seguin 1912, and with merger became Texas Lutheran College.

On the vacated Round Rock campus, Lutheran Welfare Society on Oct. 9, 1929, opened Trinity Lutheran Homes, to care for children and aged persons. Today, 1972, only one of the former college buildings still survives.

The building was 147 ft. long, 60 ft. wide with the wings on either side 40 ft. wide.

Dr. J. A. Stamline's starting salary as first President was $1,200.00 annually. Fees for the first school year were as follows: Room rent in the building, 50 cents a week; board in the college dining room, $2.50 a week and tuition was $1.25 a week.

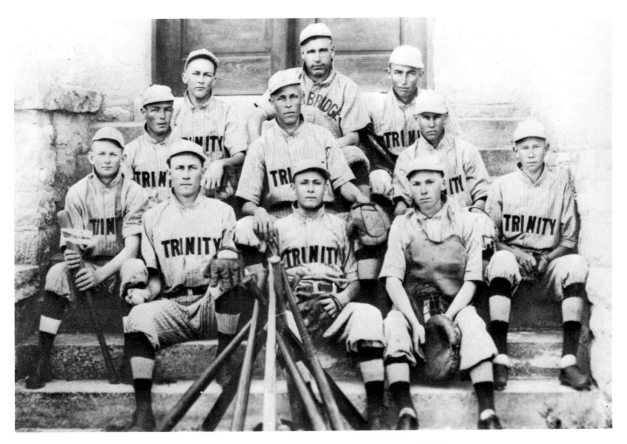

THE 1915-16 TRINITY COLLEGE BASEBALL TEAM

Front—Art Lind, Bud (Oliver) Carlson, Willie Parker.
Middle—Robert Westberg, Oscar Lundelius, Reuben Gustafson, Gunnar Jacobson, John Anderson.
Back—Helmer Johnson, N. O. Hultgren, Truett Archer.

THE 1915-16 TRINITY COLLEGE BASKETBALL

Front—Helmer Johnson, Willie Spong, Reuben Gustafson, Hilding Johnson, Willie Parker.
Back—Art Lind, Coach N. O. Hultgren, Oscar Lundelius.

BOTH PICTURES WERE MADE IN 1905 IN FRONT OF THE OLD POST OFFICE WHERE THE MASONIC BUILDING IS. The two wheel rural route mail hacks made the country side all directions from Round Rock. Top mail carrier on left is Bob Carlson, father of Carlo and Leon Carlson. Postmaster Robert Hyland, 1897 until 1911, has on the derby hat. Others not identified.

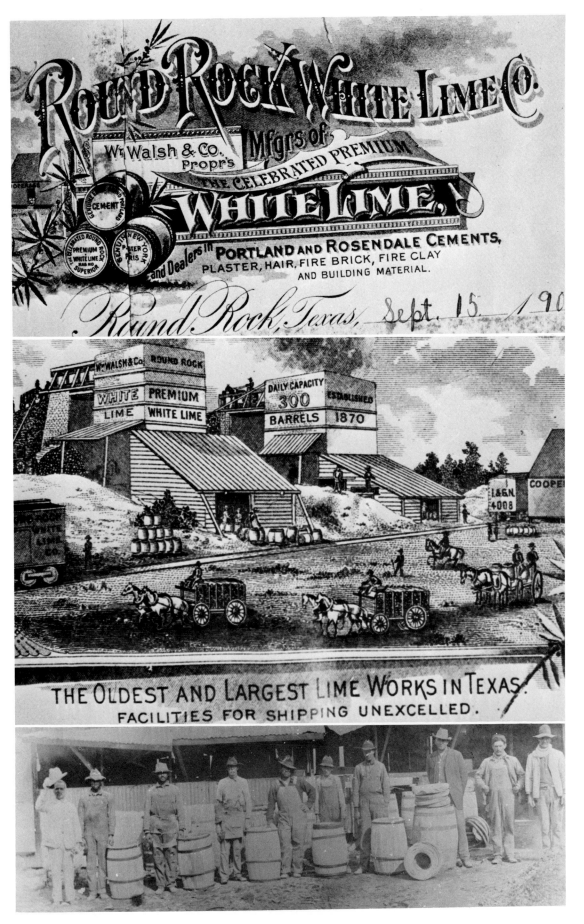

THE MERCANTILE

The Mercantile was one of the most prominent stores on Main Street in the early 1900's. This picture was made in 1917. FRONT: Jack Jordan, Elmer Black, Skeet Thorp. BACK: James Carlson, Mrs. Emma Peterson and Eric Swenson.

COMPLIMENTS OF INEZ NELSON, OLIVER "BUD" CARLSON AND JOHN JORDAN

Interior of the S. A. Pennington Jewelry Store at 105 East Main Street in 1907.

W. J. FOUSE LIVERY & FEED STABLE in 1911 on West Main St. L. to R.: Henry Pards, Jeff Fouse, Dewey Bradford, unknown, and Bud Grumbles.

A group of young business men about 1907. Front: Walter Henna, Wallace Bradford and H. L. Stockbridge. Back row: John Hyland, Norman Egger and Skeet Thorp.

J. A. NELSON & CO., A PRIVATE BANK

THE J. A. Nelson Bank was started in 1900 before the days of bank examiners and state regulations. Mr. Gus R. Lundelius went to work here in 1913. He is standing in the teller window and Mr. Carl Nelson is standing in the door.

FARMERS STATE BANK

The Farmers State Bank was chartered in July of 1920 and opened for business in August of 1920, in the building now occupied by the Texas Power and Light Co. Mr. A. W. Klattenhoff and Gus R. Lundelius stand in front of the building that housed the bank until it moved to its present location in 1960.

COMPLIMENTS OF TOM E. NELSON, JR.

Interior of the J. A. Nelson Hardware store in 1900 when the store opened. Picture on left shows the "appliance" section, bank part of building on the right.

L. to R.: Unknown, Martin Moses (barber) Austin Pennington (jeweler), W. J. Walsh (owner) Archie Hester and Luke Robertson. Rest unknown. On Right: Store on Bagdad Street.

Interior of the W. J. Walsh Store in 1907. Picture on left L. to R.: W. J. Walsh, Owner. Jim Sharp, Mr. Stanley and H. L. Stockbridge. People on right unidentified.

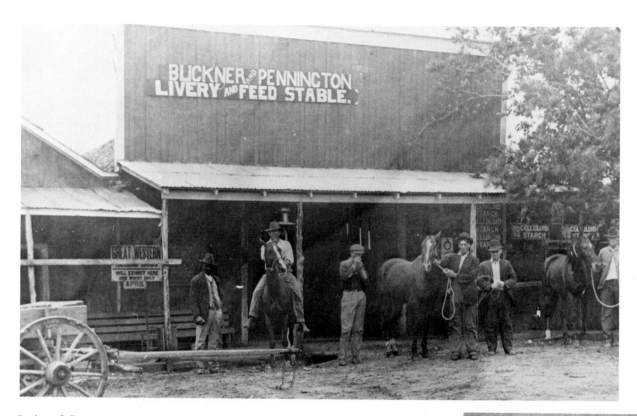

Buckner & Pennington Livery and Feed Stable in 1916. Bud Parks on horse, Dewey Long, Marshall Ferrell, Claude Buckner, Sr., and Dud Pennington. Located in 100 block of West Main St.

Dud Pennington in the 1915 horse-drawn taxi. Operated out of the Buckner and Pennington Livery and Feed Stable.

1914 CHAMPIONSHIP GIRLS BASKETBALL TEAM
Front: Jewell Sanders, Thelma Gage, Clara Daniels, Stella Baker. Middle: Eva Mae Ledbetter, Vera Jester, Gertrude Ganzert, Lola Taylor, Violet Sanders and Edra Anderson. Back: Lorraine Voigt, Katie Studer, Coach Thomas Ferguson, Nettie Bradley and Lou Pennington.

1911 BASEBALL TEAM—Front: W. A. Truesdel, Posey Awalt, Jack Jordan, Coach, John Trusdel and Bert Fouse. Back Row: Curtis Parker, Leslie Parker, Merrell Jester, Lloyd Landrum and Gill Foyil.

Mr. H. N. "Farmer" Egger and Curtis Parker with a 1913 ice delivery wagon. Horse-drawn wagons delivered ice for home and business use.

The Anderson-Nelson Company in 1910. Jim Carlson, Ima Peterson, A. Katy Anderson and J. A. Nelson in picture. Located in same building where Arden Johnson's Store is.

THE LEANDER MILLEGAN LIVERY STABLE

Pictured on left is in front of the Leander Millegan Stable in the 100 Block of West Main. Mr. Millegan owned and operated this business from 1919 until 1937.

With Mr. Millegan: L. to R.: Grandchildren, Jack Millegan, Dorthy Mae Whitley, Velma Lee Millegan and Jewell Barrnett.

Picture lower left is of Mr. Leander Millegan taken in 1929.

Picture below is of Mrs. Leander Millegan and Velma Lee Millegan and dog Queen. Picture made in 1920.

COMPLIMENTS OF MRS. O. C. WHITELEY
GEORGETOWN, TEXAS

RUTLEDGE, TEXAS—1920. A town non-existent was some 8 miles West of Round Rock. Waiting to catch the train into Austin. L. to R.: Alex Warren, Maggie Warren, Ima Warren, Nancy Whitaker, Matilda Whitaker, Lizzy Warren, Maggie Whitaker and Thompson Warren.

COMPLIMENTS OF MRS. BUDDY THOMAS

GRANT MILLEGAN, ROSCOE AND STANLEY as they display their skunk, 'possum and ring-tail coon hides and their days catch to skin and sell for money.

COMPLIMENTS OF GRANT MILLEGAN

Mr. Charles W. Prewitt standing with his horse-drawn mail buggy in 1917. Mr. Prewitt carried mail on Route 1 from 1916 to his retirement in 1941. On cold days, Mr. Prewitt would take an old pot-bellied stove with him in the buggy to keep warm. Large rattlesnakes were a common sight in the woodlands west of Round Rock he served.

Mr. Edward Peterson with his Model A that he used from 1928 until retirement in 1960. Mr. "Ed" started carrying mail in 1923 using a gig when it was dry and on horseback when it rained. He graduated to the Model "T" in 1923.

Top picture is the Pollard Motor Company about 1920. Middle picture is the Round Rock Motor Company about 1930 with the TWENTY MILLIONTH FORD on display!

HARRY L. STOCKBRIDGE GROCERY STORE in 1918. Was located in the Old Harris Building. Tomanet Corp. now occupies this building. Johnnie McDonald and Viola Stockbridge on left with Harry L. Stockbridge in front.

COMPLIMENTS OF H. L. STOCKBRIDGE

WALTER BIEL—Telegrapher & Clerk at the Round Rock Railroad Depot from 1912-1924. In addition to his regular duties, Mr. Biel handled express, baggage and sold tickets. During his years at the station, the highlight of the day for the entire community was to meet the train and see just who was coming and going. Tickets to Austin cost 40 cents and roundtrip 75 cents. On Saturdays, some 30 to 50 people would catch the train to Austin.

COMPLIMENTS OF MR. WALTER BIEL

33

WOODMEN OF THE WORLD GROUP. L. to R.: Skete Thorp, Mr. Mills, E. W. Swenson, Charley Robertson, Jack Lynn Bradley, O. L. Brady, Leonard Hall, Bud Killen, Bud Grumbles, Fred Caswell, Jeff Fouse, Lee McDonald and Walter Henna in hack.

COMPLIMENTS OF ROUND ROCK MOTOR COMPANY

Mr. Robert Egger with a load of winter fuel. This was the method of getting the winter supply of wood for both heating and cooking. This load came from the Herbert Ganzert Ranch west of Round Rock in the year 1922.

COMPLIMENTS OF
CENTEX BUTANE CO.
Georgetown, Austin, Taylor
and Florence.

ROUND ROCK CHEESE FACTORY ON A 1928 morning when farmers were bringing their milk cans on every type of car and truck. This was a $100,000.00 business in its first year of operation. In 1929, the cheese factory paid farmers $15,000.00 a month which was some two-thirds of the total payroll of the town. Mr. A. H. Kaufman was manager.

COMPLIMENTS OF A. H. KAUFMAN

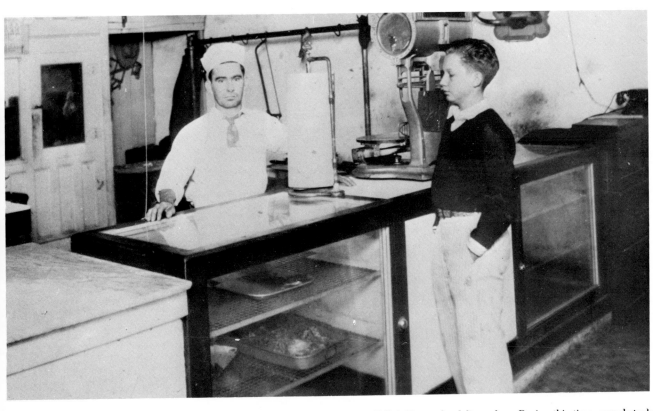

CITY MEAT MARKET in the early 1930's. Elmer Hester butcher with Wilbur (Billy) Henna the delivery boy. During this time, round steak sold for 15 cents per pound or 2 lbs. for 25 cents.

COMPLIMENTS OF GAIL HESTER

TOMMY HARBERT, DELIVERY MAN FOR VOIGT & BRADY GROCERY STORE

VOIGT & BRADY GROCERIES—Morris Ledbetter and Lex Voigt stand at the side of store in the early 1920's. The store was formerly occupied by W. J. Walsh and today is occupied by Kelly Cleaners.

COMPLIMENTS OF COCA-COLA—DR. PEPPER BOTTLING CO.
AUSTIN, TEXAS

HOYT CRIMM GROCERY on Main Street in 1936. L. to R.: Enos Martinez, John Hester, Johnny Burk, Hoyt Crimm, Tom McNeese and Pete Champion.

CITY MEAT MARKET in 1937. Henry Daffern, Owner.
COMPLIMENTS OF TAYLOR MEAT COMPANY
Charlie and Van Zimmerhanzel, Prop.
Taylor, Texas

WORLD'S LARGEST ROAD SIGN

This sign was built in 1938 just south of Round Rock on property owned by Mr. Ernest Anderson. The site was due west from where the Leigh Motor Company is now. The vast size of the sign, 47 x 107 feet, with 16,610 board feet of lumber, can be seen by comparing the size of the 1937 Chevrolet in front of the sign.

This sign was built by the C. W. Berryman Co. who was associated with the Henna Motor Company for many years. Mr. Berryman is now deceased.

MRS. MOODY MAYFIELD, clerk-cashier, stands behind a modern Texas Power & Light Co. display in 1930.

Cody Adolphson with his 1929 T.P.&L. truck. T.P.&L. began serving customers 9-15-27.

Cody Adolphson with his service truck on retirement, 9-30-68 after 41 yrs. service.

Texas Power & Light Company demonstrates a new method of feed grinding with an electric motor to a group of Round Rock farmers in 1929.

1947 Fireman's Banquet at S & S Grill

Top: Walter Henna, J. W. Ledbetter, C. V. Lansberry, & Jack Jordan.

Middle: Dr. D. B. Gregg, Mayor W. W. Rucker, Rev. French and J. H. Kavanaugh.

Right: Cody Adolphson and Brady Anderson.

EARLY 1950's PICTURE HONORING PAST WORSHIPFUL MASTERS OF MASONIC LODGE 227
FRONT: Walter Henna, Fred Olson, L. O. Ramsey, J. N. Johnson, J. T. Hutto.
MIDDLE: Murray Deison, Hoyt Crimm, Floyd Carlson, Moody Mayfield, Gene Woods.
BACK: Joe C. Parker, C. V. Lansberry, Gilbert Everett, Martin Anderson, Cody Adolphson.

COMPLIMENTS OF MRS. M. O. DEISON, HOYT CRIMM AND FLOYD CARLSON

1947 FIRE DEPT. BANQUET. SEATED: Wallace Ledbetter, Jack Jordan, Oliver Carlson, M. O. Deison, Roy McMurtrie, Bill Fyke, H. L. Stockbridge, Reynold Berglund, Wallace Rucker, W. W. Rucker, L. O. Ramsey, C. D. Anderson, Larue Mackemson, Fred Olson, C. V. Lansberry, Walter Henna. STANDING: Pete Hester, Leroy Behrens, Leroy Forrest, O. T. Bengtson, Sr., Dick Mayfield, Dr. D. B. Gregg, Peaches Ferrell, Robert L. Egger, Charles Boatner, Charles Brotherman, Cody Adolphson, and Brady Anderson.

41

1940 ROUND ROCK GIRLS SOFTBALL TEAM SPONSORED BY CLAY POT CAFE

FRONT: Fayrene Parks, Marie Robinson, Jean Jennings, Loraine Parker, Minnie King. BACK: Monk Pearson (Manager), Amanada Ponder, Royleen Teague, Velda Hill, Artie Ferrell, Lerlene Womble, Mary Opel McCann and Bill Hill, Coach.

COMPLIMENTS OF JEAN JENNINGS BUSTIN AND LERLENE WOMBLE WARD

1941-42 JUNIOR CLASS. FRONT: Marilyn Boatright, Eva Mae Dailey, Jessie Bingham, Estell Byrom, Willie Bernice Warren, Virginia Noren, Jean Jennings. MIDDLE: LaVerne Sims, Hubert Millegan, Bud Thompson, Leroy Petterson, Tom Moore, Leslie Forsman, John Wallace Ledbetter, W. O. Warren, John Edward "Bud" Warren. BACK: Cecil Toungate, Leonard Zimmerman, Chester Johnson, Tubby Ferrell, David Brice, Billy Schmidt, Arnold Snygg, Malcom Williamson. Mrs. Thomas, Sponsor.

COMPLIMENTS OF W. F. "BUB" ADAMS SERVICE STATION

PIONEER FAMILIES

Mr. "Roe" (Edward Rodolphus) Parker and wife, Lillie Briggs Parker, settled in Round Rock about 1884. He established a freight line between Round Rock and Austin and other nearby towns and did all kinds of hauling by use of wagon and both two and four horse teams.

Mrs. Parker taught piano lessons. They were active members in the Christian church and reared a family of eight children, six of whom were born in Round Rock. These children were Sam, Perle, Leslie, Curtis, Nannie, Stella, Margaret, and Cecil. The living members of this family in 1972 are Leslie, Stella and Cecil.

There is one surviving descendant of this family who has been a Round Rock citizen for many years. Mrs. Edward "Tiny" McNeese (Thelma Parker) was born in Merrelltown and was the daughter of Sam Parker and the first grandchild of Mr. and Mrs. Roe Parker.

This picture was taken in 1908 in Austin. Father and mother, Mr. and Mrs. A. E. Lundelius seated. Standing L. to R.: Oscar E. Lundelius of Houston, Ernest Lundelius of Austin, Carl Lundelius, Gus R. Lundelius of Round Rock, Ann Lundelius of San Antonio, seated Olga Lundelius Seth of Kerrville, Bertha Lundelius Foster of Austin, Signe Lundelius Poetter of San Antonio and Roland Lundelius of Houston. The Lundelius family came to Round Rock in the early 1870's.

JOHN D. AND CAMBY CAHILL FAMILY
1853-1938   1863-1939

This 1909 picture was made at the Cahill home in McNeil, Texas.
Back Row: Mike, Tom, Jim and wife Bessie, Fred and Albert.
Front Row: Jack, Joe, Mrs. Cahill, George, Mr. Cahill, Henry and Jasper.

THE WILLIAM A. TRUSDEL FAMILY

The William A. Trusdel family moved from Giddings, Texas to a farm and ranch two miles northwest of Round Rock, settling here in 1899. This prominent family consisting of seven girls and three boys, farmed and raised cattle in this area for over fifty years.
FRONT: L. to R.: Olevia, Mrs. Alice Olevia Trusdel, Awalt, Mr. William Alonzo Trusdel, and W. A. Trusdel, Jr. BACK: Irene, Ethel, Bessie, John, Daisy, Mattie and Ella.

THE CHARLES D. FULKES, SR. FAMILY

The Charles D. Fulkes, Sr. family settled near Round Rock in 1905.
Front: Charles D. Fulkes, Sr., Daisy Dell, Mrs. Besse Fulkes. BACK: Mary and Charles D. Fulkes, Jr. and the two children on left: Loucrecia and Rose.

JOHN AND BETTY PETERSON   THEIR CHILDREN: LILLIE AND NINA

Mr. John Peterson arrived in Round Rock, Texas from Norway in the early 1870's. He was the first blacksmith in Round Rock. He built his shop on West Main St. Miss Betty Olson also arrived in Round Rock from Norway in the early 1870's. They were married July 24, 1880 in Georgetown by Pastor J. J. Bruce. Two daughters were born to this couple; Mrs. Lillie Peterson who died in 1969 and Mrs. Nina Peterson who died in Everitt, Washington. They had 10 grandchildren, 6 great-grandchildren and several great, great grandchildren. Descendants include Mrs. Raymond Sellstrom, Linda Cummings and son Ray lives in Round Rock. Hilding Peterson, Austin, Texas; Roy and Lawrence Peterson of Leander; Arnold Peterson and Mrs. Rosie Richardson of Corpus Christi and Mrs. Myrtle Perry of Everitt, Wash.

In the early 1880's disaster struck when fire burned an entire block of business houses including Mr. Peterson's blacksmith shop and home. He then moved across the street with his business.

Mr. Peterson died in 1906 and Mrs. Peterson died in 1887. They were members of Palm Valley Lutheran Church and are buried in the Palm Valley Cemetery.

THIS PAGE COMPLIMENTS OF MR. & MRS. RAYMOND SELLSTROM

CAPTAIN JAMES BARNETT KEMP 1833-1881

Home of Capt. James B. Kemp, built in 1870 in Merrelltown and burned in 1904. He was a Merrelltown farmer, owned and operated blacksmith shop and a horse powered gin. L. to R.: Minnie Kemp, Fronia Kemp, Rev. Harmon, Lillie Kemp, Daisy Kemp & Sam Kemp.

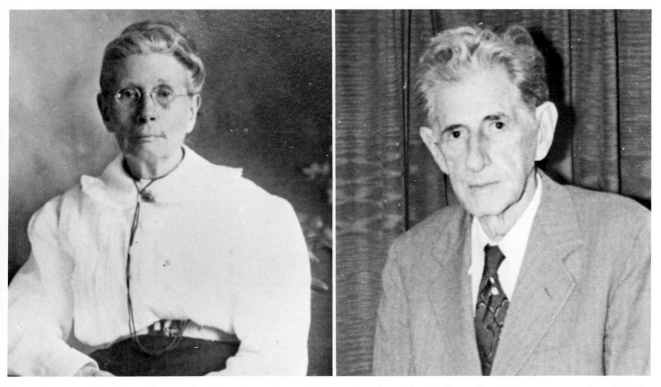

Pictured above is Mrs. Fronia Kemp, wife of Capt. James Barnett Kemp, and mother of Sam B. Kemp. Sam B. Kemp was a member of the first graduating class of Round Rock school in 1894 with his wife-to-be Mary Hope, later a school teacher. Sam Kemp was a tax collector, county judge in Coke County, served on the Supreme Court of Hawaii, later Chief Justice and Governor of Hawaii.

COMPLIMENTS OF MR. AND MRS. TOM KEMP AND MR. AND MRS. WILLIE KEMP

THE C. W. PETERSON FAMILY. This family came to Round Rock in 1876 and settled in the Palm Valley Community. FRONT: Blanche, Mr. C. W. Peterson, Edmond, Herbert, Mrs. Ellen Peterson, Lambert. BACK: Ebba, Alfie, Clarence, Lillie and Amy.

COMPLIMENTS OF MR. AND MRS. HERBERT L. PETERSON

THE J. M. JESTER FAMILY

This family picture was made in 1937.
SEATED: J. M. Jester and Mary Merrell Jester.
STANDING: John Biel, Vera, Baily, Susie and Merrell.

DANIEL F. FOUSE AND MARY CROMWELL FOUSE

Came to Round Rock in 1900.

COMPLIMENTS OF MRS. ELNA FOUSE CRUMLEY

CAPTAIN NELSON MERRELL BUILT THIS HOME IN 1870

Standing in front of home L. to R.: John E. Merrell, William Merrell, Mrs. Martha Jane Merrell, (Mother), Dudley Merrell and Nelson Merrell. The home is on Highway 79 just east of Round Rock.

COMPLIMENTS OF MR. AND MRS. JOHN E. MERRELL, JR.

EDGAR AND ETHEL MILES
Twin Children of

SAM J. MILES

The miles family owned and operated a store in Old Town in the same building that the Mays and Black Store was in. They lived in the back of the store.

COMPLIMENTS OF DEAN MILES
WACO, TEXAS

ROUND ROCK INSTITUTE
SIXTEENTH ANNUAL CATALOGUE
ANNOUNCEMENT FOR 1899-1900

Round Rock is a pleasant little town situated between Austin and Taylor on the I&GN Railroad, at the point of intersection of the Georgetown Branch of this road.

It has about one thousand inhabitants and is noted for its health and morality. It contains nine churches and not a saloon, and its surrounding productive farms, abundance of pure water, its elevation above sea level, its moral and high-toned citizenship, its Church and Sunday School facilities, its railroad telephone and telegraph communications with all parts of the country render it a most desireable place for one among the best of high schools.

The High School building is a splendid modern two story structure situated in the center of an eminent campus between the old and new parts of town, and about one half mile from the business street. The rooms are nicely finished, well ventilated, adequately furnished with maps, globes, charts, and blackboards, and commodious to accommodate all who may attend.

The school grounds comprising several acres are well fenced, and every provision is made to cause it to be a most attractive site for a school building.

Round Rock has been for a number of years a High School that ranged second to none in this section of the state, giving their children a liberal education at home without the expense of sending elsewhere for it. The school now begins its 16th annual session since its organization as a High School, with a scholastic enrollment of two hundred and fifty pupils.

Some changes have been made in the faculty this term. The Board deems it appropriate to write a few words of introduction concerning the new members. We have employed Prof. J. B. Bird to succeed Prof. O. A. Stubbs as Principal. Prof. Bird is a thorough scholar with a first grade State Certificate and has had ten years experience as Principal. He is a thorough disciplinarian and while we are not running a reformatory, those having either boys or girls that have not been controlled heretofore are especially solicited to give our school a try.

Miss Sarah Engstrand will have charge of the 4th and 5th grades. Miss Nora Hudson has been retained as teacher of the 2nd and 3rd grades. Mrs. M. E. Cunningham has again been secured as teacher of the primary grades.

Trustees are: J. W. Ledbetter, Sec'y.; J. A. Nelson, and J. M. Jester.

RULES AND REGULATIONS: 1. Every pupil is required to be punctual and regular in attendance, diligent in study, courteous to teachers, kind and obliging to schoolmates, and to refrain from the use of profane and obscene language, to be neat and clean in person and dress. 2. No pupil afflicted with a contagious disease, or coming from a house where such a disease is known to exist, shall be permitted to enter or remain in school. 3. The use of tobacco in any manner whatever, either in school or recess, is strictly forbidden, except by written permission of parent or guardian, and then during recess only. 4. Any pupil damaging or defacing any part of the school property shall pay full damages before being re-admitted to the school. 5. Pupils shall go directly to and from school and abstain from all playing and quarrelling on their way. 6. Communications between the opposite sexes is strictly forbidden. The boys will be required to occupy one side of the grounds and the girls the other. A violation of this rule will subject the pupil to suspension for the first offense and expulsion for the second.

The tuition fees for non-scholastic age pupils and those not belonging to this district, shall be $1.50 for underage and $2.50 for overage. Those unable to pay tuition will be admitted free, providing application is first made to the board. Parents are earnestly requested to be mild in their criticism, to visit the school as often as possible and give us their hearty support and cooperation.

The above summary of the 1899-1900 ROUND ROCK INSTITUTE SIXTEENTH ANNUAL CATALOGUE is only in part. The Kiwanis Club wishes to thank Mrs. A. J. Crumley for making this historical document available.

FIRST GRADUATING CLASS OF THE ROUND ROCK PUBLIC SCHOOL IN 1894
FRONT ROW: Elmer Rowe, Lura Halley, Blanche Wiess, May Hope, John Hall.
MIDDLE: Professor Hale, Grace Crutcher, Joe Walker, Hilda Engstrand, and Sam Kemp.
BACK: Jeff Palm, Hallie Holloway, Susie McDonald and Henry Palm.

GRADUATION CLASS OF 1913. This was the last class to graduate from the first public school before it burned. FRONT: Mildred Jackson, Katy Studer, LaNella Chambers.
SECOND ROW: Stella Parker, Mamie Morgan, Rosa Olson, Inez Jordan, Mamie Gray.
THIRD ROW: Hattie Taylor, Vander Broadway, Prof. M. G. York, Chester Jackson, George Johns.
BACK: Bailey Jester, Roy Wright, Cecil Thorp, Cecil Cochran and Wallace Ledbetter.

1903 CLASS. FRONT: Robert Egger, Fritz Caswell, Bascomb Bradley, Elmer Gustafson, Carl Johnson, Reggie Royal, unknown. MIDDLE: Matilda Ganzert, Wanda Dody, Mildred Johnson, Emma Johnson, Ruth Stones, Edith Pearson, Ellen Blair. BACK: Freda Johnson, Minnie Johnson, unknown, Louise Falwell, teacher, Earl Cockran and Paul Pokrant. Mr. Clinkscale was the janitor, firebuilder and water drawer.

FRONT: Lorraine Voigt, Oscar Stewart, George Stone, Paul Landrum, Ralph Johns and Robert Egger. MIDDLE: Nettie Bradley, Elvra Pearson, Ruth Stone, Emma Johnson, Lola Taylor, Clara Daniels. BACK: Arthur (Peaches) Ferrell, Paul Pokrant, Carl Wright, Margaret Palm, Ida Roberson and Professor Webb.

COMPLIMENTS OF MR. AND MRS. ROBERT L. EGGER

1907 PALM VALLEY SCHOOL PICTURE

Front Row: Oscar Warner, Agnes Quick, Walter Noren, Jessie Dabs.
Second Row: Annie Peterson, Enna Johnson, Margaret Palm, Signe Quick, Alma Quick, Ebba Quick, Elsie Johnson & Edith Burklund.
Third Row: Lillie Johnson, Eric Swenson, Oscar Beck, Tilda Palm (Teacher), Louise Johnson, Hugo Swenson, Jack Anderson, & Oscar Burk.
Back Row: Bertha Johnson, Nels Swenson, Ellen Noren, Nora Pokrant, James Harris, George Harris and Don Dabs.

This picture dedicated to Mr. Harry Noren

Round Rock High School 1914-1959

SENIOR CLASS OF RRHS 1921. FRONT: Oscar Quick, Ellen Anderson, Cora Hester, W. E. Cantrell, Supt., W. R. Woolsey, Principal, Ruby Parsons, Lester Wright, Monroe Black. MIDDLE: Thelma Mohrman, Zenia Voigt, Nelson Johns, Stanley Christopherson, Elmer Johnson, Ima Taylor, Ellen Hester. BACK: Alief Halton, Mae Robertson, Edwin "Carlo" Carlson, Hubert Sanders and Marion Hammer.

1926 GRADUATION CLASS: FRONT: Valerie Stockbridge, Mamie Behrens and Lorene Crimm. BACK: C. D. Fulkes, Bernie Ferrell and Moody Mayfield.

1925 ROUND ROCK HIGH SCHOOL FOOTBALL TEAM. FRONT: Garland Walsh, Ott Voigt, Bernie Ferrell, LeeRoy Lewis, Roger Burleson MIDDLE: Bub Allen, Johnnie Robertson, Clarence Quick, "Porky" Bradley, Mascot, C. D. Fulkes, Eugene Loving, Moody Mayfield and Dick Jordan. BACK: Boyce Crimm, Butter Bradley, Allen Bradley, Gordon Gant, Chester Allen and Coach Tull.

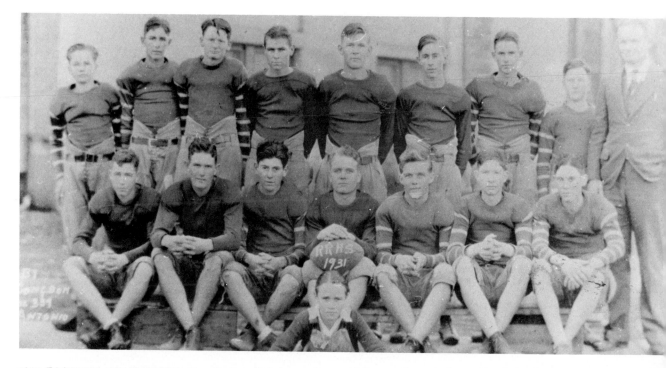

1931 FOOTBALL TEAM. FRONT: Tiny Bradley, S. C. Inman, Raymond Sansom, Leon Anderson, Martin Linder, Mack Trusdel, J. R. Gill, Jack McCann, Mascot. BACK: Wilbur (Billy) Henna, Gene Inman, Jack (Red) Carlson, Leon Behrens, Otto Linder, Harry Robertson, Noel Inman, John (Porky) Bradley and Mr. O. F. Perry.

1932 SENIORS. FRONT: Blanche Hill, Bill Kavanaugh, Bernice Anderson, Elizabeth Kavanaugh, Otto Linder, Marie Hester. MIDDLE: Billy Schmidt, Frank Fouse, Onie Dettenhaim, Belinda Berklund, Helen Frisk and Holly Sandlin. BACK: Mr. C. O. Britt, E. J. Walsh, J. R. Gill, S. C. Inman, Jack (Red) Carlson, and Harry Robertson.

HOPEWELL SCHOOL IN 1930-31
Principal W. H. Lamkin and B. L. Bradshaw and W. E. Mercer, Teachers

Grades 4 & 5, May 21, 1930. FRONT: Luther Earl Ferrell, Jack McCann, Rinie Zimmerman, Warren Piland, Forsman, Marvin Anderson, Raymond Davis, Leslie Sullivan. SECOND: Charlotte Kavanaugh, Hill, Vernette Kaufman, Frances Sellstrom, June Walsh, Thelma Mae Smothers, Unknown, Thelma Lois Schmidt, Doris Egger, Jessie Ruth Bradley, Laura Anderson. THIRD: Imogene Wilson, Mary Killen, Anita Robertson, Mary Opal Warren, Willie Mae Egger, Unknown, Rosemary Hall, Dorthy Madsen, Feliz Pena, Gentry, Blanche Blad, Georgia Lee Hickman. FOURTH: Mrs. Lambert Nelson, F. W. Ferrell, Alvin Youngblood, Virgil Anderson, Unknown, Emory Pokrant, Carles Prewitt, Sammy Loving and P. E. Dickson.

COMPLIMENTS OF MR. & MRS. R. L. EGGER

1937 GRADUATION CLASS. FRONT: Florence Belk, Edith Parker, June Walsh, Vernette Kaufman. MIDDLE: Thelma Schmidt, Jack McCann, Doris Egger, Dorthy Madsen, Charlotte Kavanaugh, Imogene Wilson, Geneva Johnson, Georgia Lee Hickman, Laura Anderson. BACK: August Peterson, J. C. Woodson, Charles Prewitt, Raymond Davis, Luther Earl Ferrell, Spurgeon Britt, Joel Johnson.

COMPLIMENTS OF CLASS MEMBERS

FIRST BAND OF ROUND ROCK HIGH SCHOOL 1941-42. MAJORETTES: Virginia Noren, Bonnie Burk. DRUM MAJOR: Bernice Kathryn Ledbetter. BAND DIRECTOR: Milton Dusek. FIRST ROW: John Wallace Ledbetter, Virginia Richards, Hartley Berkman, Joe D. Anderson, Eva Mae Daily, Nan Ledbetter. SECOND: Cecil Toungate, Bessie Mae Reeves, Laura Jean Pearson, Irene Ferrell, Doris Archer, Regina Walsh, Margaret Kavanaugh, Betty Landrum. THIRD: Mike Olson, Joe Henna, Ella Mae Anderson, Genevie Klattenhoff, Alvin Wilson, Moody Anderson. BACK ROW: Buddy Perry, Velda Ruth Hill, Buddy Lee, Carolyn Peterson and Martha Lou Perry.

1941-42 PEP SQUAD. CHEERLEADERS: Betsy Ross, Jean Jennings, Ruby Williams. MASCOTS: Edward Mercer and Tommy Nelson. L. to R.: Margaret Adams, Beulah Beth Warren, unknown, Inez Anderson, Gloria Sellstrom, Cora Mae Fields, Lillie Dell Adams, unknown, unknown, Nadine Ferrell, Betty Jo Ferrell, unknown, Marion Boatright, Fannie Fay Fields, Willie Bernice Warren, Martha Thompson, Lillian Zimmerman, Louise Warren, Pat Pierce.

1939 FOOTBALL TEAM. FRONT: Lawrence Scott, Wallace Rucker, Douglas Cahill, Ira Hester, John Wallace Ledbetter, Mascot, Charles Jennings, Calvin Blacklock, Howard Anderson, Arden Johnson, Joe Egger. MIDDLE ROW: Warren Kaufman, Chester Johnson, George Woolsey, Joe Parker, Luther Ross, Robert Moehring, Victor Robertson, Milton Ferrell, Emory Johnson, Larue McLaurin. BACK ROW: Coach Black, Chester Jacobson, Frank McNeese, Bill Inman, Arthur Lee Ferrell, Milton Krienke, Alton Prewitt, Coach Henson and O. F. Perry, Supt.

1941-42 DISTRICT CHAMPS. FRONT: Hilary Wilson, Bill Walsh, Bud Thompson, W. O. Warren, Cecil Holloway, S. A. Womble, Leslie McNeese. SECOND ROW: Douglas Cahill, Eric Anderson, Tom Moore, Jack Daniel, Stanley Maynard, Bud Warren, Roland Warner. BACK ROW: Mr. O. F. Perry, Joe Egger, Chester Johnson, Milton "Tubby" Ferrell, Calvin Blacklock, Malcom Williamson, Aaron Lee Gill and O. V. McDaniel, Coach.

1939 PEP SQUAD, Miss McVey, Sponsor. FRONT: Mary Sansom, Ellen Pearson, Gladys Anderson, Laverne Bingham, Marilyn Boatright, Jean Jennings, Lerlene Womble, Betty Jane Prewitt, Kathryn Blacklock, Regina Walsh, Grace Cahill, Blanche Telander, Bernice Kathryn Ledbetter, Margaret Cahill, Virginia Noren, Betty Landrum. BACK ROW: Doris Berkman, Octavine Trusdel, Pauline Robertson, Elizabeth Harris, Marcella Johnson, Frances McNeese, Bertha Snygg, Billie Jean Forest, Ruby Williams, Nadine Ferrell, Johnnie Ross, Dorthy Bustin, Wilson, Maxine Inman, Fields, Marilyn Houston, Mary Frances Warren, Edith Harris, Amanda Ponder, Dorthy Walsh, Betty Jo Ferrell, Willie Bernice Warren, Loraine Parker and Lillian Johnson, Cheerleaders: Marjorie Johnson, Dorthy Collier and Lillianette McNeese. Mascots: Betty Johnson and other unidentified.

1937 FOOTBALL TEAM—C. O. Britt, Supt. and O. F. Perry, Coach. FRONT ROW: Leroy Behrens, Luther Ross, Gilbert McNeese, Lynnwood Fredrick, Floyd Anderson and Walter Zimmerman. MIDDLE: Bill Hill, John Loving, Edward McNeese, Winfred Anderson, and Wilbur (Snow) Johnson. BACK: Bill Inman, Kenneth Goode, Bobby Henna, Frank McNeese and Haywood Fredrick. S. A. Womble, Mascot.

COMPLIMENTS OF ROOSTER ANDREWS SPORTING GOODS, INS. AUSTIN, TEXAS

61

1963 23-A CHAMPS

FRONT: James Sargent, Teddy Behrens, Charles Johnson, Jr., John Hernandez, S. C. Inman, Jan Jordan, Jerry Jordan, Terry Williams, Guy Kercheville. MIDDLE: Larry Toungate, Bobby Davis, Harry Robertson, Jr., Wayne Warren, Jimmy Morgan, Theo DeLaRosa, John Zamarippa, Gene Toungate, Clifton Baccus. BACK: Ernest Dailey, Billy Allen, Eddie Johnson, Johnny Moore, Jim Sherrill, Robert Carlin, Bobby Moore, Bobby Cheramie, Ricky Allen, Ronnie Harrison. COACHES: Charles Nelson, Jim Dodson, Jerry Davis, Lee Frasier.

COMPLIMENTS OF JOHN J. JORDAN

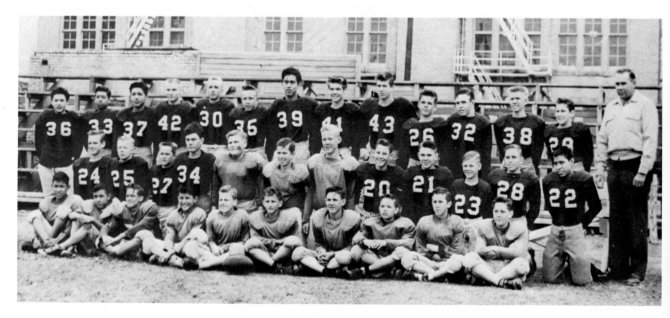

1956 ROUND ROCK JUNIOR HIGH FOOTBALL TEAM

FRONT: Jose Avila, Florentino Hernandez, Edward Chambers, Jessie Avila, Robert Ryle, Sandy Langfield, Bobby Langefeld, Tommy Kelley, Henry Bradley, Clarence McKenzie. MIDDLE: Calvin Black, Gene Hensley, J. H. Cantwell, Charles Ward, Jackie Neans, John Burnett, Tommy Jones, Robert Kosler, Theo Zimmerman, Jr., Benny Sargent, Jerry Crain, Mike Martinez. BACK: Joe Lozano, Henry Nava, Vincente Perez, Thomas Pruett, Vernon Stidham, Lloyd Sellstrom, Martias Diaz, Gene Mayes, Marvin Glascock, Phil Graham, Marvin Gilbert, Buddy Guess, Tony Womble and Coach Arnold Peterson.

COMPLIMENTS OF MEMBERS OF THE TEAM

OUTSTANDING EX-STUDENT

C. D. Fulkes on left receives an award plaque as the outstanding ex-student of Round Rock High School at the Homecoming game 1971. The award was presented by Noel Grisham, Superintendent of Schools, during halftime ceremonies at the Homecoming game with Elgin. Mr. Fulkes graduated from Round Rock High School in 1926 and returned to serve as teacher and High School Principal from 1950 to 1971.

MEMORIALS

Jack Jordan

1872–1959

Jessie E. Jordan

1873–1951

Jack Jordan and his wife Jessie Jordan on their 50th wedding anniversary, December 31, 1946.

Jack Jordan, born in Bell County on September 7, 1872 and married to Jessie Elizabeth Thorpe of McNeil, and moved to Round Rock in 1906.

Mr. Jordan was a member of the First Baptist Church of Round Rock where he taught a Sunday School class for thirty years. He was the first Mayor of Round Rock in 1913 and became City Secretary of Round Rock in 1914, which post he held until his retirement in 1958. He was the first president of the Round Rock Chamber of Commerce. He was a member of the Round Rock School Board for several years prior to 1916.

At the time of his death, he was survived by one daughter, Mrs. Inez Nelson; two sons, John M. Jordan and Dick T. Jordan; five grandchildren—Betty Jo Peterson, daughter of LeRoy and Inez Nelson, Dick T. Jordan, Jr., and Robert Neal Jordan, sons of Dick T. & Verna Dean Jordan, Jan A. and Jerry S. Jordan, sons of John M. and Laverne Jordan.

Dick Bolling Gregg, M.D.

Doctor Gregg came to Round Rock to practice medicine as a general practitioner in 1921. In 1926, he married Zelma Presler of Florence, Texas, then a school teacher in Round Rock schools. One daughter, Mrs. Susan Barton, is living in Middlebury, Va.

Doctor Gregg was a typical country Dr. He called on the sick in all directions from Round Rock, any hour of the day or night, willing to be of service to everybody. Dr. Gregg received many honors during his 42 years of practice in Round Rock, and was loved and cherished by all his friends. He truly helped mold Round Rock into the growing community it is today.

Walter E. Henna

Mr. Henna was born in Austin and came to Round Rock in 1902. He was married to Maudie Morgan and their four sons, Louis M., Wilbur E., Robert L., and Joe B. all grew up in Round Rock. Mr. Henna was a community leader and successful business man. He was a lumber and hardware dealer, real estate broker and gas and oil dealer. Mr. Henna was active in the Williamson County O.S.A., Round Rock Cemetery Association, County School Board, Masonic Lodge 227, Chamber of Commerce and First Baptist Church. He was named an "Outstanding Citizen" by the Chamber of Commerce.

Mr. Henna was a gentleman, a model husband and father and a real friend to all who met and knew him.

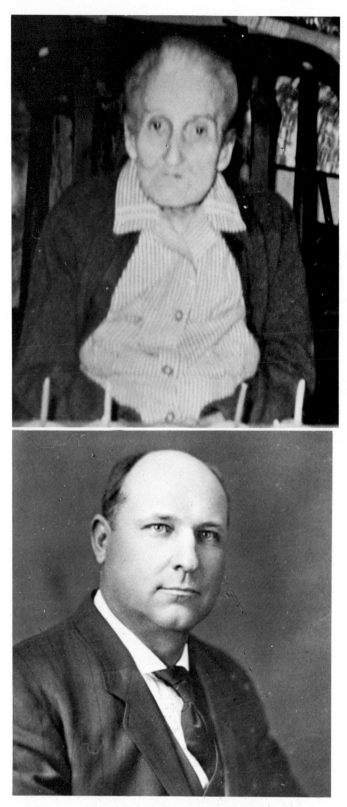

Ida York

September 2, 1873–December 28, 1967

Mrs. York was born in Glasgow, Kentucky and moved to Texas at the age of three. They settled near Grayson and Fannin County line and then moved to Hill County near Itasca. Mrs. York saw the coming of the MK&T (Katy). She was teaching in Itasca when she met her husband-to-be, Mr. M. G. York. They moved to Round Rock in August of 1907. They had 4 children, and were active members of the First Baptist Church. One of her delights in her later years was watching the comings and goings of Principal C. T. Berkman about the Central Elementary School. Their son, Manor York, is still a resident of Round Rock.

John A. Nelson   Jenny Carlson Nelson

John A. Nelson, born to a pioneer Williamson County family in 1866, married Jenny Carlson and settled in Round Rock in 1869. He became prominent in local business, founding the John A. Nelson Co. and, with others, a band, the Mercantile Company and the Broom Factory. The family was active in the Palm Valley Lutheran Church, and Mr. Nelson was highly instrumental in bringing Trinity College to Round Rock. The Nelsons had six children—Edith, LeRoy, Lambert, Lillian, Vivienne, and Ansel. They lived in Round Rock until their death. Mr. Nelson in 1922 and Mrs. Nelson in 1946.

Thomas Edward Nelson

February 7, 1888–December 15, 1951

Thomas E. Nelson was born and reared on the family farm five miles north of Round Rock. His father, Andrew J. Nelson, and mother, Hedvig Nelson, emigrated from Sweden to America in 1856, and were pioneer colonizers who helped turn the wilderness into a prosperous farming and stock raising country.

Mr. Nelson was educated at Ford's Academy, Austin, Texas, Bethany College, Lindsborg, Kansas, and the University of Texas. He served as an officer in the U.S. Army and for three years was private secretary to Congressman J. P. Buchanan of the Tenth Texas District in Washington, D. C. He was a founder and the first president of the Farmers State Bank in Round Rock and was associated with his brother, Carl A. Nelson, in various farming and business ventures including the Round Rock Cheese Company. In 1929, he married Rebecca Young Schofield, who survives him and lives in Austin. His son, Thomas E. Nelson, Jr., is presently associated with the Farmers State Bank of Round Rock.

Tom Nelson was a member of Palm Valley Lutheran Church, which his father helped build. He loved the Round Rock community and was vitally concerned with the problems of his friends and neighbors. He served as a member of the City Council and Treasurer of the school board.

Brent Bustin

January 6, 1950–November 2, 1969

Outstanding Round Rock Youth
in sports and academics . . . .
a young leader in the community

The Brent Bustin Memorial Park just west of Interstate 35 is named in his honor . . . .

Served as Round Rock Fire Department's first Mascot and was named State Mascot at the State Firemen and Fire Marshals' Association 1955-1956 . . . .

The State Firemen and Fire Marshals' Convention dedicated in Brent Bustin's Memory 1970 . . . .

Scholarships instituted in memory include The Firemen's Memorial Scholarship and the Brent Bustin Memorial Scholarship . . . .

Attended Round Rock Schools and Southwest Texas State College.

Edward John Walsh

Edward John Walsh was born January 19, 1890 to William and Dora Walsh in Austin, Texas. In 1908, after the death of his father, he assumed the responsibility of President and General Manager of the Round Rock White Lime Company, which position he held until 1949 when the Lime Company was sold to Joe Bland, et al.

"Mr. Ed", as he was known to everyone passed away April 7, 1962.

Josie J. Aten
- Frank Lincoln Aten

1860-1960   1869-1951

Mr. Frank L. Aten was born in Peoria County, Illinois. Mr. Aten came to Round Rock in 1876. Mrs. Aten was born in Saltville, Virginia and came to Round Rock in 1882. Mr. & Mrs. Aten were married in Austin, Texas in 1886. They had six children. Mr. Aten was charter member of the Williamson County OSA. He was postmaster at Round Rock from 1922 until 1931. For many years Mr. Aten was a bee keeper in Round Rock. He shipped the first car load of honey ever produced by one man out of Texas in 1897.

John W. Ledbetter

1896-1968

John W. Ledbetter was born in Old Round Rock July 10, 1896. Was Postmaster at Round Rock many years. Served as school trustee and Scout Leader. Was a deacon in First Baptist Church. Belonged to Masonic Lodge 227. Was a member of American Legion. Received Chamber of Commerce award as Outstanding Citizen. Served as president of Round Rock Fire Department. Was President of Williamson County Old Settlers Association.

Rev. Theo Krienke

1896-1956

Rev. Theo Krienke was a graduate of Texas Lutheran College, Seguin, Texas and Lutheran Theological Seminary, Dubuque, Iowa. He came to Williamson County in 1912 and served several congregations in this area. In 1929, he moved to Round Rock with his wife and two children to become the first Superintendent of Trinity Lutheran Homes and served both aged and children for sixteen years. After serving two years as a trustee of the Round Rock School Board, Rev. Krienke was elected president and held that office for twenty years. From February 1934 until February 1954.

Children: Milton, Karl, Roland, Robert, Roy and Ruth. All are graduates of Round Rock H. S.

Carolena Nelson Palm   Andrew Palm

Andrew Palm was born in Sweden December 20, 1839. He passed away in Palm Valley, Texas November 8, 1928.

Carolena Nelson Palm was born November 17, 1851 in Sweden. She passed away on August 20, 1929.

They were married in Palm Valley, January 7, 1875.

Mr. and Mrs. Otto A. Voigt

1871-1953   1869-1962

Mr. Voigt was born in Hawley, Pennsylvania December 19, 1871. He came to Texas as a young man. He was married to Isabelle Engstrand in 1898. He was in the Tinning and Plumbing business for more than fifty years.

Mrs. Voigt was born in Austin, Texas, August 13, 1869. She was a Charter (infant) Member of the Palm Valley Lutheran Church. She was also a Charter Member of the Round Rock P.T.A. and served faithfully in the organization for many years.

Their children, Lorraine, Alexius, Arno, Xenia, Kathleen, and Ott, were all born and reared in Round Rock.

Lorraine M. Voigt

1899-1971

Lorraine, the daughter of Mr. and Mrs. Otto A. Voigt, was born and reared in Round Rock. She was active in religious and civic organizations. She worked in the Round Rock Post Office, and as bookkeeper for The Mercantile and The Ford Motor Company. She retired from active duties as Vice-President and Cashier of the Farmers State Bank in January, 1969 after serving in that capacity for thirty years.

Charles V. Lansberry

1891-1971

Mr. Lansberry was born in Franklin, Texas and attended school at Trinity High School and the University of Texas. He was admitted to the State Bar to practice law in 1917. He served in WWI in France and returned to serve as a lawyer in Round Rock from 1924 until his death. He served as assistant District Attorney for Williamson County 1929-35. Also served as city attorney of Round Rock. Mr. Lansberry served in the Texas Legislative from 1941-46. He was a member of Masonic Lodge 227 and the First Baptist Church of Round Rock.

John Herring Kavanaugh

November 9, 1879
January 8, 1957

Mr. Kavanaugh was owner, editor and publisher of Round Rock Leader for 27 years. "Our Column," widely read, expressed his opinion on all subjects, especially politics. Previously published papers in five other towns. Former school teacher and merchant. Native of Woodville, Texas. Steward in Methodist Church 45 years, Royal Arch Mason, Charter member Round Rock Kiwanis Club, member of Chamber of Commerce. This is a 1955 photo.

Carl Eric Quick

1910-1971

Carl Eric Quick was born October 29, 1910 to Mr. and Mrs. P. A. Quick. Eric attended Round Rock Public Schools and Trinity College. He was employed at the Round Rock Ice Company for six years and at the Round Rock Post Office for 28 years. He was a veteran of World War II, serving with the U.S. Navy.

Eric married the former Carmen Johnson on June 2, 1935. Their daughter, Norma Jean, was born December 27, 1936.

Eric was a lifetime member of the Palm Valley Lutheran Church.

Bill Lyle Kavanaugh

1916-1963

Bill Kavanaugh was born in Richland Springs, Texas, April 14, 1916. He attended and graduated from Round Rock as salutatorian of his class in 1933.

He volunteered for the Army in 1941, was commissioned an Infantry Lieutenant, and at the time of his death, was a Lieutenant Colonel in the 36th Division of the Texas National Guard.

After receiving his law degree from the University of Texas at Austin in 1950, he entered private practice of law in Round Rock. Later was assistant county attorney, before accepting a position with the Texas Dept. of Public Safety and became legal counsel of the department.

He was Past Master of the Masonic Lodge No. 227, Past Adjutant of George Johns Post No. 447 and a member of the Methodist Church, the Williamson County Bar Asso. and the State Bar of Texas.

Edgar Vaught

1885-1968

Mr. Edgar Vaught was born September 23, 1885. He was married to Alma Williams of Austin in 1921.

Mr. Vaught came to Round Rock in 1936 and soon went to work with Henna Motor Company and was associated with that company until his death.

He was a member of the Chamber of Commerce, Kiwanis Club, Member of the Odd Fellows, and the Methodist Church.

He was a great fisherman.

Felix M. Ferrell, Sr.

1860-1944

Felix M. Ferrell, Sr. was born January 30, 1860 and came to Round Rock in 1870 from Grapeland, Texas. He married Edna Earl McCain in 1888. He was a farmer, butcher, carpenter, and was appointed nightwatchman of Round Rock in 1918 and held that position until his retirement.

His children were: LaUna, Marshall, Waymon, Arthur, Lola, Avery and Bernie.

Luke Robertson

1876-1970

"Uncle" Luke Robertson spent his entire 94 years in Round Rock. His grandfather, Luke S. Robertson came to Williamson County in 1843 from Missouri where Mr. Luke's father, John D., was born. Mr. Luke saw the first barbed wire, the first cultivator and the first commercial flour in sacks to arrive in Williamson County and he also saw the State Capitol being built. He attended school before there were free schools in Texas. He was well known for his dough-bait for carp fishing and was quite a fisherman himself. Anyone wanting information on Historical facts would go to him as his memory was excellent. He was in the General Merchandise business in Round Rock for 42 years.

Mr. Edward Othella Maxey
Mrs. Florence Verna Maxey

1894-1969   1898-1970

Mr. and Mrs. Maxey were married August 18, 1915, and they moved to Round Rock in 1942. Mr. Maxey was born at Mud, Texas, which is now the entrance to Paleface Park. Mrs. Maxey was born at Travis Peak. Mr. Maxey was a retired real estate agent and they had six children: Emalee, Mildred, Kitty, Cricket, Ross and Shug.

D. B. Lane

1876-1959

Mr. Lane was born in Bastrop County and was married to Ila Humphries in 1900. He came to Round Rock in 1929. He built Lane Courts and Service Station in 1935. Mr. Lane was a successful business man with business interest in Round Rock, Elgin, Hutto, Austin, and Marble Falls. He was a director of the Farmers State Bank, a rancher, and a member of the Masonic Lodge. His son Durwood lives in Round Rock and daughter Beulah Lane Meadows in Austin.

Murry O. Dieson

Murry Deison came to Round Rock in 1923 and was employed by the Walsh Bros. at The Round Rock White Lime Co. as bookkeeper for over twenty years. He started the M. O. Deison Insurance Agency in 1926, and was married to Velma Miller in 1928.

In 1944 he was employed by the Farmers State Bank and served as its president from 1945 to 1955. After that he devoted his full time to his insurance business until his death in 1959. He served on the City Council, assisted in the organization of the Kiwanis Club, was very civic minded, and an ardent sportsman.

William Jefferson Fouse

1883-1936

William Jefferson Fouse was born in Paris, Mississippi and came to Round Rock in 1900. Married Susie Jester in 1907. Worked at the Broom Factory, hauled wood, loaded gravel, owned store in Old Town, gins, rock crusher, livery stable, steam grain thresher, hobby horses, railroad team gangs, farms, and milk routes. Sold real estate and insurance. Active member Volunteer Fire Department, Woodmen of the World, I.O.O.F., Methodist Church, O.S.A., Liberty Bond and Red Cross Drives.

Trustee at Stony Point School.

Children: Elna (Mrs. A. J. Crumley), Frank 1915-1952.

W. S. "Buster" Brown

1852-1947

Mr. Brown was born at Webberville, Texas, January 30, 1852, and moved to Round Rock in 1910. He was soon elected one of the towns earliest mayors in 1914. He was very active in civic affairs, a natural poet and a deeply religious layman of the Baptist Church. His daughter, Mrs. Durwood Lane is a resident of Round Rock.

MUNICIPAL GOVERNMENT

Present Mayor, Dale Hester, 1969-1972

Mayor Elmer A. Cottrell, 1965-1968

Mayor Martin Anderson, 1961-1964

Mayor Edward J. Walsh, Jr., 1957-1960

Mayor Louis M. Henna, 1952-1956

Mayor W. W. Rucker, 1943-1949

1972 CITY COUNCIL OF ROUND ROCK

Raymond E. Litton, James D. Toungate, Dale Hester, Mayor, Garfield W. McConico, Marcelo R. Beltran and Gene A. Parker.

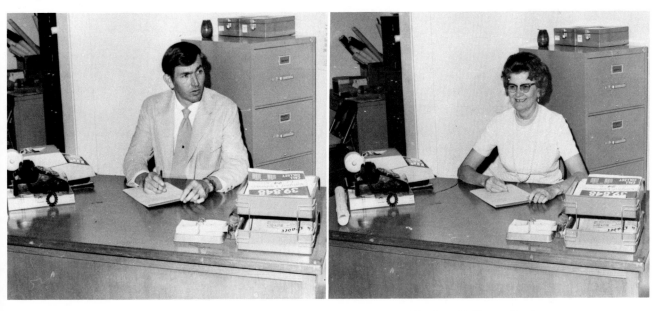

Willis R. Stafford,   City Manager   Mrs. Oscar E. Nauert, City Secretary

1947 CITY COUNCIL OF ROUND ROCK
FRONT: Tom E. Nelson, Sr., W. W. Rucker, Mayor, Charles V. Lansberry, City Attorney. BACK: Jack Jordan, City Secretary, C. D. Anderson, Murray Deison, Louis M. Henna.

CITY FATHERS VISIT BERGSTROM A.F.B. IN 1957
L. to R.: Elmer Cottrell, Martin "Doc" Anderson, L. O. Ramsey, Arden Johnson, Harry Robertson, Mayor Edward J. Walsh, Jr., Rudolph Petersen and Eddie Burk.

ROUND ROCK FIRE DEPARTMENT 1972

RONT: Robert Behrens, Cody Adolphson, Paul Jones, Bob Bairrington, J. B. Johnson, Robert Griffith, Jack Swinden, David Leppin, Glen ehrens, O. T. Bengtson, Sr., O. T. Bengtson, Jr., Bennie Bustin, Ted Galloway, Johnnie Roepke, Roy Krienke (Insert). BACK: Alan Boutwell, tewart Rohre, Moody Mayfield, Elmer Hester, Raymond Sellstrom, Delfino Torres, Charles Gunby, Darrell Swinden, Oliver Leppin, Sr., C. J. winden, John Collins and Oliver Leppin, Jr. Absent: Sterling Mitchell and Theo Zimmerman.

OFFICERS AND TRUCK CAPTAINS OF THE ROUND ROCK FIRE DEPARTMENT IN FRONT OF CITY HALL. L. to R.: Captain J. B. Johnson, truck #4, Cody Adolphson, Fire Chief & Fire Marshal, Raymond Sellstrom, Captain, truck #1 (in truck), Jack Swinden, (Mascot), C. J. Swinden, 2nd Assistant Chief, O. T. Bengtson, Jr., Captain, truck #2, John Collins, Captain, truck #3 and Stewart Rohre, Vice President.

WITH COMPLIMENTS AND THANKS TO THE ROUND ROCK FIRE DEPARTMENT
H. STEINFINK, J. OTIS AND E. STEINFINK

Dud E. Stone

1876-1967

Mr. Dud, as he was better known, was nigh watchman from 1942 until 1965.

While most merchants slept, Mr. Dud woul make the rounds, looking into stores, checkin doors and watching for fires as well as fc burglars.

Punching the clock was a way of life for M Dud.

Cody Adolphson

FIRE CHIEF & FIRE MARSHAL

Cody joined the Round Rock Fire Department in March of 1925. He served as President and has been Fire Chief since 1943 and has been both Fire Chief and Fire Marshal since 1969.

He served as President of Central Texas Volunteer Fireman's Assn. in 1960-1961. Is presently serving as Sec.-Treasurer Williamson County Fire Chiefs Association.

Records have been kept since 1943 and the Round Rock Fire Department has answered 1330 alarms from 1943 thru 1971. Cody has answered 1104 of the 1330 alarms. He has noticed a great increase in alarms in his 47 years.

1949 FIRE DEPARTMENT MEMBERS

FRONT: Carl Eric Quick, Roy McMurtrie, Cody Adolphson, Fred Olson, John W. Ledbetter,
MIDDLE: Charles Brotherman, Bill Kavanaugh, Guy Inman, Bennie Bustin, Moody Mayfield,
BACK: Brady Anderson, Leroy Forrest, Raymond Sellstrom, Raymond Johnson, Reynold Berglund.

RETIRED MEMBERS OF THE 1949 ROUND ROCK FIRE DEPARTMENT

FRONT: John Sunden, Harry L. Stockbridge, C. D. Anderson, Oliver "Bud" Carlson.
BACK: John E. Merrell, Jr., Luther O. Ramsey and Walter E. Henna.

Waymon Ferrell

Born September 22, 1894 to Felix and Edna Ferrell. Spent his entire life in Round Rock with the exception of 3 or 4 years. Married Artie Scott and was night watchman for many years. Was also constable for 6 years. Then again night watchman and Chief of Police for several years.

He and Mrs. Ferrell operated a small cafe where the Central Elementary School is now.

Mr. and Mrs.
Felix M. Ferrell, Sr.

Mr. Ferrell was night watchman from 1913 until his retirement.

84

Waymon Ferrell at Sam Bass grave site.

Above picture is of the ROUND ROCK HOOK AND LADDER CO. purchased in 1907 for $700.00 Names of members not available but charter members of HOSE COMPANY organized in 1900: A. Bradley, J. K. Cooker, Jas. Walsh, Seth Sullivan, R. M. Crimm, Ernest Matteson, H. V. Sunden, J. E. Jenkins, Wm. Sisk, J. E. Sullivan, Lawrence Stone, W. B. Bradley, Charles L. Bustin. THE HOOK AND LADDER COMPANY was organized in 1907. Names of members of Round Rock Volunteer Fire Dept. from 1907 to 1917 as follows: M. L. Blacklock, T. W. Mayfield, A. W. Engstrand, R. L. McDonald, E. R. Carlson, Clark Buckner, O. A. Voigt, B. J. Mayfield, E. M. Black, L. Sodberg, Fritz Caswell, A. W. Blad, A. K. Anderson, J. A. Holloway, W. E. Henna, H. W. Ganzert, W. J. Fouse, B. H. Allen, H. L. Stockbridge, S. Bradley, L. T. Cole and O. L. Brady.

ROUND ROCK GIRLS PUMPER TEAM

Picture on the left was taken from the June 1, 1941 Texas Fireman. It was the first Girls Pumper Team in the state of Texas. This team was organized in 1941 by H. L. Stockbridge, when most all of the boys went into the service. When first organized, these girls went all over Texas making exhibition runs. They started something for now several of the Fire Departments have girls pumper teams who compete the same as the men's teams do.

FRONT: Olene Stockbridge, Velda Ruth Hill and Jean Jennings.

BACK: Lerlene Womble, Artie Louise Ferrell and Marie Robinson.

CHURCHES

Come Worship With Us

Pond Springs Baptist Church

Jollyville, Texas

Serving since 1932
        —Faithfully ministering 40 years for the Lord.
Growing with the community.
        —Membership has doubled in past three years.
Expanding to meet the needs.
        —$55,000.00 spent on additions and improvements last year.
Teaching the Word of God.
        —All activities are Biblical centered.
Ministering to all people.
        —Reaching out in Christ's name.

        Sunday Schedule is as follows:
                9:45 A.M. Sunday School
                11:00 A.M. Morning Worship
                6:30 P.M. Bible Study and Choir Programs
                7:30 P.M. Evening Worship

                        Rev. John Rudd, Pastor
                James A. Kirk, Minister of Music and Youth

ST. WILLIAMS CATHOLIC CHURCH

St. William was established in 1940 by The Holy Cross Fathers. Since 1964, it has been an independent Parish, with Fr. Fred Schmidt as its first Pastor. Plans are to build a new church within 2 years.

ON RIGHT: Father J. Dona, the first Catholic priest to serve the church in Round Rock in 1916. He came from Austin every Sunday.

LOWER RIGHT: The house of Francisco Carlin in 1939, located near Lime Factory. Was used for holding religious services from 1916 to 1940. Mr. Carlin was the first to bring a priest to Round Rock for religious services.

LOWER LEFT: Fr. Rosendo Rafael, the present Pastor. There are 1,300 Catholics in Round Rock and Leander Parish.

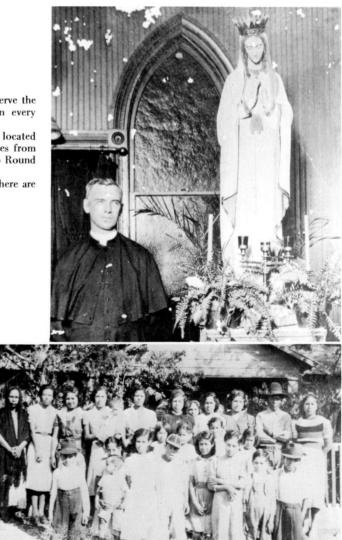

ABOVE: The present building for the church was started under the Pastorate of Rev. Don Lillejdahl and completed with Rev. Lewis Sommermeyer as Pastor. Opening services were held on August 31, 1958. RIGHT: Old Church Building.

THE ROUND ROCK METHODIST CHURCH

The Round Rock Methodist Church was dedicated on Sunday morning, April 6, 1879. A special train brought four car loads of visitors from Georgetown for this occasion. The Consecration sermon was given by the Rev. R. T. Nabors of Houston. The Pastor was the Rev. B. S. Lane in 1879. Rev. G. W. Graves served as a circuit rider for both Round Rock and Georgetown in 1877 and 1878.

ABOVE: The church parsonage, next to the church, was built in 1965 with Rev. Dale Hunt as Pastor.
LEFT: The present Pastor, Rev. George Matthews.
BELOW: The old parsonage of the church.

The Round Rock Church of Christ Salutes You

Salute one another with an holy kiss. The churches of Christ salute you.
Romans 16:16

And if you salute your brethren only, what do you more than others? do not even the publicans so?

St. Matthew 5:47

Elders

E. J. Davee, Jr.   W. R. Stafford

Deacons

Franklin Anderson   Robert L. Reed

"And let these also first be proved; then let them use the office of a deacon."
1 Tim. 3:10

Evangelist

N. E. Balch

"Do the work of an evangelist, make full proof of thy ministry."
2 Tim. 4:5

Through the ministry of Raymond Gentle, the church was first established in Round Rock during the summer of 1933. A band of 16 Christians met for worship in the tabernacle at Old Settlers Grounds until the cold of winter forced them to seek new quarters. The group then moved to the City Hall. Later a meeting house was built. The State Highway department selected the site of this house of worship as a part of a new highway system in 1957. The present facility was erected and occupied in 1958. Classrooms were added in 1969. The first Vacation Bible School was held July, 1970. First elders and deacons were selected in Oct., 1970. "Round Rock Reminder" first mailed to community April, 1970.

All scripture is given by inspiration of God, and is profitable for doctrine, for reproof for correction, for instruction in righteousness: That the man of God may be perfect, throughly furnished unto all good works. 2 Timothy 3:16&17

The Church of Christ in Round Rock uses this picture of the format of the "Round Rock Reminder" which is published weekly as a community service and may be received on request. The Bible on the round rock is symbolic of our prayer for Round Rock—That God's word will be elevated to have supreme authority in our lives. Then, and only then, will we "keep the unity of the Spirit in the bond of peace." See Eph. 4:1ff.

"But Jesus said, Suffer little children, and forbid them not, to come unto me: for of such is the kingdom of heaven." St. Matthew 19:14

Every year, (usually the last week in July), the church has Vacation Bible School for everyone in the community. The first one began in July, 1970 with well over 100 students. The second year, (of which the 2 & 3 year olds and the 3rd & 4th grades are shown), had well over 150 students.

FIRST BAPTIST CHURCH

BOB PARKER, PASTOR

JOHN 3:16
For God so loved the world, that he gave his only begotten Son, that whosoever believeth in him should not perish, but have everlasting life.

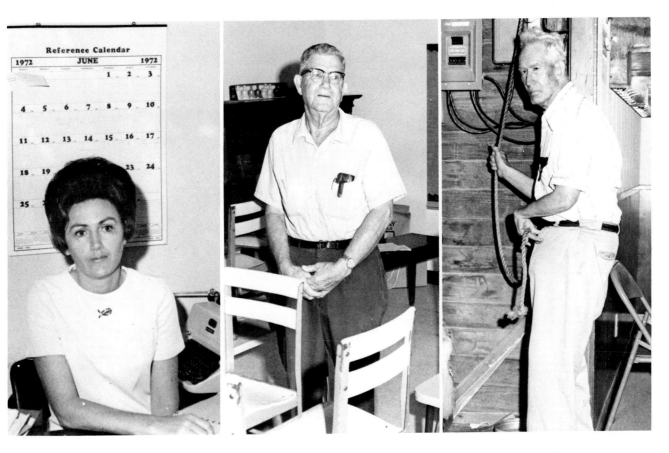

JOYCE McCOY, SECRETARY   CECIL HUDSON, CUSTODIAN   MANER YORK

FIRST BAPTIST CHURCH
202 North Brown Street

The First Baptist Church at Round Rock was founded in 1854 as the Brushy Creek Baptist Church. The church has been known as: Brushy Creek Baptist (1854-1857), Old Round Rock Baptist (1858-1891), Round Rock Baptist (1892-1917), Robertson Memorial Baptist (1917-1948) and First Baptist (1948-1972).

The church has been a member of the following associations: Union (1854-1855), Little River (1855-1857), Austin (1858-1920) and Williamson (1921-1972).

Worship services have been held in the present church since 1921.

The church has had the following pastors since 1918:

Rev. J. C. Mitchell	1918-1926
Rev. H. G. Sloan	1926-1928
Rev. Buford Nichols	1929-1933
Rev. George Green	1933-1940
Rev. H. D. Dollahite	1941-1944
Rev. M. L. Richards	1944-1945
Rev. Jimmy Bolton	1946-1949
Rev. O. E. Simpson	1949-1950
Rev. J. R. Heller	1951-1954
Rev. J. J. Jordon	1955-1958
Rev. R. D. Hendricks	1958-1959
Rev. James Janeway	1960-1963
Rev. Everett Martin	1963-1964
Rev. James D. Watson	1965-1972
Rev. Bob Parker	1972

FIRST BAPTIST CHURCH CHOIR, DWIGHT LAMB, DIRECTOR

FRONT: Carolyn Woods, Pat Kramer, Sue Livingston, Nancy Lamb.
MIDDLE: Virginia Woods, Vera Scott, Dwight Lamb, Barbara Hudgins, Margaret Carlson.
BACK: John Powell, Terry Parker, Martin E. Parker, Carlton Scott, Cecil Hudson, Jimmy Cardova, Clifford May.

NAN LEDBETTER ANTILL
ORGANIST

SUE LEIGH
PIANIST

FIRST BAPTIST CHURCH KINDERGARTEN

BOTTOM ROW: Heath Martin, Carl Krueger, Stacy Moore, Carmen Crider, Jo Ann Salazar, Connie Inman. SECOND ROW: Hunter Anderson, Randy Row, Lisa Simcik, Mike Bairrington, Ron Simpson, Kathy Valenta, Jimmy Toungate. BACK ROW: Steve Millegan, Brent Brown, Sharon Robertson, Arthur Zamarripa, Karen Kramer and Jeff McCoy.

THE BOB PARKER FAMILY—BOBBY DEAN, BOB, DOLORIS, BOBBY DWAIN

SWEETHOME BAPTIST CHURCH, REV. A. W. MAYS, PASTOR

SWEETHOME BAPTIST CHURCH CHOIR
FRONT: Joyce Estelle, Mabel Clark, Beaulah Mercer, Ora Woods, Patricia McVade, Mrs. S. L. Williams. MIDDLE ROW: Jo Anne Robinson, Lucindia Mercer, Fannie Mays, Artie Mae Schooley, Leona Anderson, Beatrice Mercer, Frances Sampson and Reverend A. W. Mays, Pastor. BACK ROW: Deacon Henry Clark, Deacon Sammuel Mercer, Deacon Wadell Mercer and Iva Mae Toliver.

96

1952 Aerial view of the TBCH Campus

Texas Baptist Children's Home

Mr. and Mrs. Louis Henna founded TEXAS BAPTIST CHILDREN'S HOME on September 5, 1950, by giving Dr. J. Howard Williams, Executive Secretary of the Baptist General Convention of Texas, the deed to the property and five buildings.

The Home has grown to include 22 buildings and to serve over 275 children a year in different programs including the campus program, foster homes, and adoptions. The campus at Round Rock cares for 100 children.

Mr. Charles I. Wright, Adminstrator, directs these services for dependent children.

BELOW: 1972 Aerial view of TBCH Campus

PALM VALLEY LUTHERAN CHURCH

IN AREA FIRST CLAIMED IN 1838 BY WHITE MEN. VALLEY BEARS NAME OF THE ANNA PALM FAMILY, 1853 SWEDISH SETTLERS. "BRUSHY", THE FIRST LUTHERAN CHURCH (OF LOGS), WAS BUILT HERE BY ANDREW JOHN NELSON AND 3 HIRED MEN IN 1861. THIS ALSO HOUSED EARLY SCHOOL.

CONGREGATION WAS FORMALLY ORGANIZED NOV. 27, 1870. SECOND CHURCH, BUILT 1872, WAS USED FOR SESSIONS OF PALM VALLEY SCHOOL.

PRESENT GOTHIC REVIVAL STYLE BUILDING WAS ERECTED IN 1894.

RECORDED TEXAS HISTORIC LANDMARK — 1970

1972 CHURCH COUNCIL

L to R: Lawrence Hester, Norman Pecht, Leslie Pecht, Richard Baker, Herbert Swenson, Weldon Burklund, Ray Woytek, Howard Wagner, Maurice Bradley, Roland Krienke, Oliver Berglund, Jimmy Wallin, Lyman Larson, Chester Madsen, Edward D. Quick, Brady Behrens, Ernest N. Johnson.

CONGREGATION AT WORSHIP

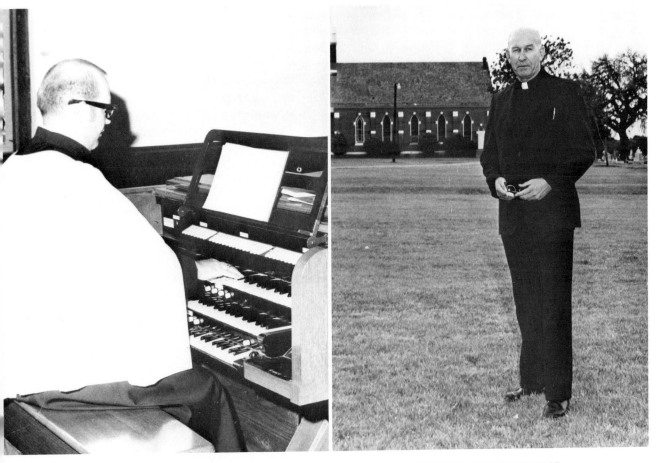

CHARLES DeLISLE, ORGANIST

OLIVER BERGLUND, PASTOR

PALM VALLEY LUTHERAN CHURCH SENIOR LUTHER LEAGUE

FRONT: Darwin Anderson, Mona Sullivan, Dana Johnson, Paul Warner, Teri Baker, Jay Baker, Cara Johnson, John Oman, Terry Frasier, and Janice Pecht.

BACK: Steve Hester, Larry Hester, Terry Walker, Larry Robertson, Alan Peterson, Paul Berglund, Stuart Whitlow, Jan Reinhardt, John Fellows and Weldon Lester.

COMPLIMENTS OF MR. AND MRS. ARNOLD PETERSON

PALM VALLEY LUTHERAN CHURCH JUNIOR LUTHER LEAGUE

FRONT: Russell Madsen, Mike Eckert, Michael Sullivan, Tia Johnson, Gary Robertson, Robbin Hester, Steve Olson, Ricky Sliva, Diane Anderson, and Greg Pecht.

BACK: Sandra Walker, Greta Prinz, Keith Krienke, Jeff Hester, Cindy Cooke, Jayne Johnson, Buddy Wuthrich, Roxanne Kaatz, Valerie Berglund and Julie Wagner.

COMPLIMENTS OF MR. AND MRS. JOE D. ANDERSON

SCHOOLS
Round Rock Independent School District

School Board: Left to Right: Bertil "Buck" Telander; E. O. Beck; Issaac Lopez, Jr.; Victor Robertson, Pres., Joan Baker; Bill Cotton; Standing: Ray Sanders; Noel Grisham, Supt.; Marvin Olson, Vice-Pres.

Central Office

Kathleen Payne, Claude Berkman, Xenia Voigt, Noel Grisham, (Honoring Xenia Voigt for her long tenure of superior service.)

Robert Behrens
Tax Assessor
Collector

Noel Grisham, Mrs. Vernell Bradley, and Mrs. Gwen Selby.

J. B. Johnson—Mgr. of Maintenance and Transportation.

Mrs. Billie Jo Reed
Tax Officer Assistant

Mrs. Ginger Springer
Mgr. of Lunch Rooms

ROUND ROCK SENIOR HIGH SCHOOL

FACULTY & STAFF

FRONT: Mary Lovett, Kathy Rolleigh, Nevalene Morsbach, Ruth Bengston, Mike Richardson, Buddy Roberts, Tommy Roberts, Ronald Kneupper, Ron Campbell, Roger Schustereit, Ike Coward, Faye Johnson, Ann Frasier, Betsy Nehring, Henry Streety.
MIDDLE: Walter Gest, Herbert Peterson, Barbara Krueger, Carol Mann, Marcia Hilsabeck, Sharon Hugele, Doyle Melton, Vonnie Tucker, Leonard Kiely, David Reinhardt, David Carlin, P. O. Brown, Henry Heisch.
BACK: Deana Fate, Pauline Madsen, Pam Brake, LaRue Samuelson, Sandra Millegan, Nell Burklund, Karen Jones, Gretelle Ekvall, Carolyn Lackey, Phyllis Henderson, Dora Martin.

Not pictured: Karen Gattis, Earl Seay, Dennis Templeton, J. B. Johnson, Jackie Gillum, Barbara Johnson, Ginger Springer.

PRINCIPAL
Robert G. Griffith

FACULTY AND STAFF OF THE MIDDLE SCHOOL

Front Row: Vivian Johnson, Jane Nugent, Betty Baker, Estella Sager, Linda Green, Ralphina Clarke, Ruth Stanford, Raymond Canizales.
Second Row: Boyd Jackson, Ann Templeton, Carolyn Weber, Mary Sloan, Hillery Canon, Bruce Southerland, Virgie Walsh, Louise Townsley, Carolyn DeLaCruz, Genevieve Berglund, George Bujnoch (Principal).
Third Row: Allen Thrower, Scott Pyle, Raymond Ganzert, Eleanor McClaferty, Gordon Franzen, Earl Klattenhoff, Thomas Millegan.
Not Pictured: Patsy Warford, Jack Saul, Ruby Bradley, and Nora Bryan.

Central Elementary School

FACULTY AND STAFF OF CENTRAL ELEMENTARY
First row: Claude Berkman, Betty Zinn, June Bredthauer, Elsa England, Edna Koehler, John Manley, Lucille Orn.
Second row: Ora Woods, Melba Hyde, Alice Rosenquest, Lillie Zamarripa, Simon Barrera, Nellene Hester.
Third row: Blanche Krienke, Pat Watson, Joe Lee Johnson, Mae Sliva, Mary Burleson, Petrenello McConico.

Southside Elementary School

FACULTY AND STAFF OF SOUTHSIDE ELEMENTARY
Back row: Left to Right: Ruth Madrigal, Lottie Butts, Agnes Quick, Ruth Stanford, Lou Peterson, Edith Sellstrom.
Front row: Left to Right: Billie Snyder, Dian Moore, Mellownie Johnson, Dian Cole, Wilma Peterson, Principal

POND SPRINGS ELEMENTARY SCHOOL
FACULTY AND STAFF
FRONT: Carolyn Douglas, Christina Schuetz, Dear Bell Crumley, Charles T. Perry, Dena Ealey, Patricia DuBois, Lucille Allen, Sec.
BACK: Vivian Lester, Fannie Blackburn, Fay Cast, Paula Purcell, Geraldine Heisch, Latrelle Thompson, Linda Grant, Linda Casbeer, and Arnold Peterson, Principal

Northside Elementary School

FACULTY AND STAFF OF NORTHSIDE ELEMENTARY SCHOOL

First row: William Earl, Ceclia Herrera, Virginia Beltran, Ollie West, Edwina Sybert, Leona Anderson, Mary Bess Harkins, LaJeanne Dupuy.
Second row: Pam Christianson, Kathleen Payne, Doris Jackson, Joyce Anderson, Delores Parker, Lanell Boyd, Marjorie Quick.

Community Clubs & Organizations

.........Kiwanis International, dedicated to the promotion of higher social, business, and professional standards, and to the development by precept and example, of a more intelligent, aggressive and serviceable citizenship, recognizes the Golden Rule as a guide for everyday life ....

THE KIWANIS CLUB OF ROUND ROCK

The Kiwanis Club of Round Rock was organized October 16, 1952 when Mr. Lewis Fouts, Governor of the Texas—Oklahoma District, presented the Charter to John Merrell, Jr., the first president of the Round Rock Kiwanis Club as pictured above.

CHARTER MEMBERS

John Merrell, Jr.	President
Jesse Todd	Vice President
Jack Hightower	Secretary

BOARD OF DIRECTORS

O. J. Carlson	Clarence Quick
Milton G. Moore	John M. Jordon
Osie M. Crain	O. V. McDaniels
E. J. Walsh, Jr.	

OTHER MEMBERS

Theo J. Zimmerman, Sr., Herbert Dollahite, Norman G. Whitlow, G. R. Lundelius, O. F. Perry, Eugene Quick, M. O. Deison Leslie Eads, Luther O. Ramsey, Claude T. Berkman, J. H. Kavanaugh, Thomas J. Moore, Darrell Blackman, Rev. O. M Bloom, Ralph Johnson, Robert E. Johnson, Vernon E. Childers, Calloway Crews, Rudolph Pettersen, Dr. D. B. Gregg, William E. Floyd and Ross Maxey.

It is through the efforts of the Kiwanis Club of Round Rock that this book is being preserved for the future generations. It would have been impossible to have this priceless document without the help of many interested citizens who are not Kiwanians. The Kiwanis Club would especially like to acknowledge Mr. Arnold Peterson who served as photographer and took some 800 to 900 pictures and gave many hours—and nights to make available the pictures you will see in this book.

Presidents who have led this organization since receiving its charter in 1952:

John E. Merrell, Jr.	1952	Joe Henna	1962
Jesse Todd	1953	Werner Keisling	1963
M. O. Deison	1954	Noel Grisham	1964
Col. W. N. Todd, Jr.	1955	W. D. Vernon	1965
Elmer A. Cottrell	1956	Mark Sheffield	1966
A. H. Lavvorn	1957	Robert G. Griffith	1967
Osie M. Crain	1958	Rev. James D. Watson	1968
C. D. Fulkes	1959	Don Hester	1969
Rev. E. Urelius	1960	W. G. McCoy	1970
Gilbert Bredthauer and		Earl Seay	1971
Osie M. Crain	1961	Martin E. Parker	1972

Glyn Morsbach has served as Secretary longer than any previous Secretary. 1969 thru 1972.

Charter members still active in the Kiwanis Club are: Robert E. Johnson, Norman G. Whitlow, Eugene Quick, Rudolph Pettersen and Osie M. Crain.

Pictured above is W. Carroll Allen, Chairman of the Boys and Girls committee and president of the Little League. On the far right is Don Hester who was president of the Kiwanis Club in 1969 when the Kiwanis Park was started. In center is Martin E. Parker, the present president of the club. Proceeds from the sale of this book will go to pay off the remaining debt on the ball fields. In 1969, the Kiwanis Club built 2 well lighted and fenced ball parks with the members doing much of the work and donated machinery and materials from several contractors. Dr. Thomas Barnett has donated some $3,000.00 to help pay on the recreation area. The two ball parks are valued at some $40,000.00. Trinity Lutheran Home made the land available.

ROUND ROCK EX-STUDENTS ASSOCIATION

The Round Rock Ex-Students Association was officially organized in 1900-1901. Reunions of students of the Pioneer Schools had been held previous to this date. From an old newspaper, we quote, "The exes of the Pioneer Schools held their second annual reunion, July 10, 1902, with Mrs. Clyde Wiess Kyle, Pres. and Mrs. Starkey Duncan, Sec. The speaker for the day was Judge W. F. Robertson. Mrs. Margaret Kenny Kress, was introduced and she expressed her gratitude for the honor and recognition shown to Dr. Kenney, the founder of Kenney's Fort, and the first settler of the county. A roll call of the exes of 1884-1885 was made by Prof. T. A. Brown."

In 1960-61, the Round Rock Ex-Students Association began a scholarship program. To this date, recepients of scholarships have been the following: Vernon Killen, Kenneth Madsen, Karen Johnson, Harry Earl Robertson, Teddy Behrens, Mary Linda Cantwell, Robert Organ, Ronnie Woytek, Pam Zimmerman, Craig Toungate and for 1972—Clara Johnson.

Oldest active Ex-Student of Round Rock High School is Mrs. LaUna Ferrell Ramsey, class of 1907.

Mr. W. R. Woolsey, a former school superintendent is still faithful in attendance and interest.

OFFICERS AND DIRECTORS
1972

Betsy Ross Nehring, Xenia Voigt, Hallie Bradley Jester, Betty Sellstrom Hester, Secretary & Treasurer, Lurlene Ramsey Merrell, President, Nan Ledbetter Antill and C. D. Fulkes, Jr., seated.

CHAPARRAL JR. WOMAN'S CLUB

The Round Rock Chaparral Club was formed and Federated in 1969. It is a member of Texas Federation of Woman's Clubs and is mainly a service club. The club has 30 members. Officers for 1972: Mrs. Dale Hester, President, Mrs. Roy Moore, Vice President, Mrs. Ted Selby, Secretary and Mrs. Gene Parker, Treasurer.

FRONT ROW: Mrs. Duwayne Sandel, Mrs. Billy Davis, Mrs. James Toungate, Mrs. Ted Selby, Mrs. Robert Behrens, Mrs. Bill Kitts, Mrs. Gene Parker, Mrs. Lee Holder, Mrs. W. G. McCoy, Mrs. Tom Newsom, Mrs. Dale Hester and Mrs. Ray Roe.

BACK ROW: Mrs. Leon Byrd, Mrs. Eddie Breaux, Mrs. Morris Noren, Mrs. Don Sanders, Mrs. Jim Peters, Miss Mildred Toungate, Mrs. Fred Henry, Mrs. Dale Park, Mrs. Bob Lehmann, Mrs. Jack Hoover, Mrs. Carroll Pimpler, Mrs. Robert Bairrington, Mrs. Roy Moore and Mrs. Ed LeClair.

NOT PICTURED: Mrs. Mike Grimes, Mrs. Larry Boyd, Mrs. George Weber and Mrs. Jerry Wall.

ROUND ROCK SWINGERS CLUB

The Round Rock Swingers Club was organized in 1967 as an Auxiliary Club of the Round Rock Woman's Federated Club. Charter officers were: Nancy Nelson, President, Carol Ruth Henna, Vice President, Beverly Johnson, Secretary, Debbie Callison, Treasurer, Linda Daniel, Reporter, Dianna Browning, Parliamentarian. Other charter members: Jerry Voigt, Jill Bredthauer, Linda Robinson, Kathy Olson, Debbie Stanford, Paula Morsbach, Teri Woytek, Janet Henna, Helen Ekvall, Susan Yates, Gayle McGilvray, Laurie Lou Parker, Nancy Walker, Judy Giesen, Kay Beck.

1972 SWINGERS CLUB

FRONT: Dana Johnson, Debbie Stork, Greta Johnson, Kathy Krienke
MIDDLE: Ann Henna, Debbie Evans, Lynn Montgomery, Jan Reinhardt, Cara Johnson, Teri Baker, Rue Ann Samuelson.
BACK: Joan Baker, Sponsor, Mary Spencer, Karen Krienke, Cindy Williams, Donna Cowan, and Cindy Walker.

OFFICERS OF ROUND ROCK SWINGERS CLUB FOR 1972

President	Greta Johnson
Vice-President	Teri Baker
Secretary	Debbie Stork
Treasurer	Joan Zimmerman
Reporter	Jeannie Heisch
Parliamentarian	Dana Johnson

Membership is from the Round Rock High School students.
Projects of the club include decorating portions of the city at Christmas, sponsoring dances for the high school students, conducting drives for UNICEF, and staging the Round Rock Beauty Pageant during Frontier Days Celebration.

The puppet Show

The Story Hour

Joyce Anderson
Nan Antill
Joan Baker
GeNelle Beck
Genevieve Berglund
June Bredthauer
Nell Burkland
Mary Burleson
Ruth Burleson
Catherine Carlson
Viola Cottrell
Laura Davol
Velma Deison
Lydia Fulkes
Ema Jean Goodrich
Zelma Gregg
Carolyn Hardin
Billie Sue Henna
Betty Hester
Faye Johnson
Nan Kelley
Edna Koehler
Clara Koontz
Blanche Krienke
Nancy Lamb
Delia Mae Lane
Bernice Ledbetter
Dorothy Ludlum
Sue Lynch
Frances McGilvray
Aliece Patterson
Kathleen Payne
Liamor Dene Pearson
Wilma Peterson
Agnes Quick
Signe Quick
Marjorie Quick
Nancy Rabb
Billye Jo Reed
Ann Robertson
Nora Rundell
Harriet Rutland
Estella Sager
June Bug Smith
Mildred Smyers
Jo Tucker
Xenia Voigt
Nevada Walsh
Alienn Warner
Geneva Whitlow

International Dinner

PROJECTS OF THE WOMAN'S CLUB

GEORGE JOHNS POST #447, ROUND ROCK, TEXAS

This American Legion Post was organized March 6, 1933. It was named in honor of GEORGE JOHNS, the first Round Rock soldier killed in World War One.

Charter members were: Carl A. Anderson, Will H. Baker, Albert E. Fields, Archie R. Franklin, Dick B. Gregg, Charles V. Lansberry, John W. Ledbetter, Gus R. Lundelius, Tom W. Mayfield, Reinhold H. Moehring, Carl E. Munson, John L. Nelson, Tom E. Nelson, George E. Peterson, Sam L. Sowell, Levie H. Thurman, Thomas A. Trusdel, Wiley R. Woolsey, Alex W. Klattenhoff.

Present Post Commander is Rudolph Pettersen, First Vice Commander, Walter T. Loewe, Post Adjuant, Adolph Hohertz, Finance Officer, Oscar T. Bengtson, Sr., Sergeant at Arms, Clarence Telander and Historian, Alex Klattenhoff.

Present members of George Johns American Legion Post #447 pictured above.

Chesley McCorkle, Walter T. Loewe, Alex W. Klattenhoff, H. Cleve Warren, Adolph Hohertz, Grover L. Kuemple, Alfred P. Reinhardt, Mrs. Bennie T. (Jean) Bustin, Oscar T. Bengtson, Sr., Rudolph Pettersen, Bennie T. Bustin, Claude T. Berkman, C. D. Fulkes and Moody Mayfield.

The first American Legion Hall was built in 1947 with Moody Mayfield Commander. The present Legion hall was built in 1958 with Moody Mayfield also the Post Commander. The first hall was built on Legion Hill which is now at the foot of North Lee Street. Present hall is at the intersection of Georgetown and E. Taylor.

GEORGE JOHNS AMERICAN LEGION AUXILIARY UNIT #447

The George Johns Unit #447 was organized in June 1950, with Jean Bustin the first President. There were 23 charter members. Charter members still active are: Jean Bustin, Annie Mae Bustin, Ruth Bengtson, Louise Lundelius, Leslie Mayfield, .urlene Merrell, Elizabeth Mikeska, and Della Trusdel.

Presently serving as officers: President, Ruth Bengtson
            1st Vice-president, Annie Mae Bustin
            2nd Vice-president, Bernice Ledbetter
            Secretary, Idell McCorkle
            Treasurer, Leslie Mayfield
            Chaplain, Katy Klattenhoff
            Historian, Agnes Quick
            Sergeant-at-Arms, Clara Hohertz

Members-at-large on the Executive Committee: Viola Johnson, Cora Warren, Della Scott.

FRONT ROW SEATED: Signe Quick, Bernice Ledbetter, Cora Warren, Annie Mae Bustin, Louise Lundelius, Katy Klattenhoff.

MIDDLE ROW: Idell McCorkle, Eleanor Pettersen, Selma Kuemple, Agnes Quick, Rosa Almquist, Clara Hohertz, Leslie Mayfield, Viola Johnson, and Vera Leowe.

BACK ROW: Gina Antill, Ruth Bengtson, Jean Bustin, Lydia Fulkes, Nan Antill and Bernice Ann Antill.

George Johns American Legion Auxiliary Unit #447 regular meetings are held on the first Tuesday evening of each month at the American Legion Hall.

THE MERRELLTOWN COMMUNITY CLUB

The second Saturday night of each month, this community club meets for fellowship and a pot luck supper. FRONT: Diane Anderson, Jimmy Parker, Rhonda Yarbrough. SECOND: Alex Klattenhoff, Frank Taylor, Vera Anderson, Joe D. Anderson, Beda Sellstrom, Martin E. Parker, Frieda Parker, Dorothy Parker, Willie Parker. THIRD: Helen M. Sherrill, Joyce Ragan, Martha McNeese, Kelcy Robinson, Rudolph Sellstrom, Katy Klattenhoff, Margaret Grosskoph, Minnie Parker, Carl F. Parker, BACK: James C. Ragan, John O. Robinson, Fred "Bill" Sherrill, Lizette Taylor, Ann Jenkins, Ed Jenkins, Arthur Grosskoph.

THE YOUNG MEN'S CLUB

The Young Men's Club was organized February 1, 1971. Gordon Woods was President. FRONT: Willie Hurd, President, Benjamin Mason, Joe Lee Johnson, Sponsor, Gordon Woods, William Earl, Sr., Sponsor. BACK: Joe L. Gadison, Parliamentarian, Charles Lee Hurd, Joe D. Johnson, Business Mgr., Sam Johnson, Asst. Treasurer, Charles Foster, Sec. & Treas. and Maurice Woods, Asst. Business Manager.

MERRELLTOWN HOME DEMONSTRATION CLUB

FRONT: Kelcy Robinson, Elva McDonald, Rose Erisman, Travis County Home Demonstration Agent, Margaret Grosskoph, Dorthy Parker, Lisette Taylor, Carolyn Schaefer, Connie Schafer, Babe Cottrell, Jimmy Morvent, Becky Richmond, Lavon Holder and Julie Holder. BACK: Mary Richmond, Vera Anderson, Esther Anderson, Lillian Lyckman, Lenora Wuthrich.

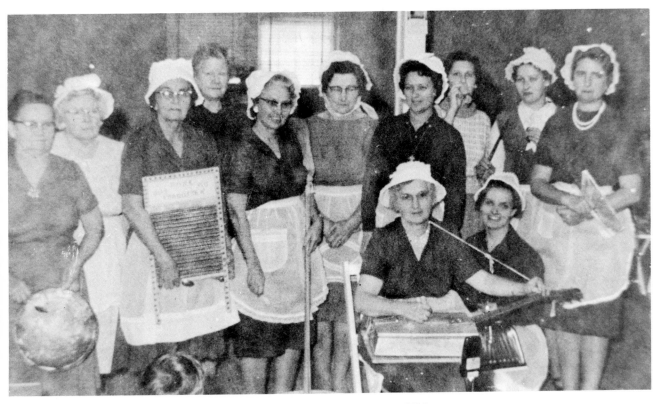

THE MERRELLTOWN MERRY MAKERS

Home Demonstration Club Band. FRONT: Dorothy Parker and Mary Robinson. BACK: Betty Glenn, Mamie Biel, Kelcy Robinson, Mrs. Ernest Allen, Sr., Lillian Lyckman, Beda Sellstrom, Frieda Parker, Darlene Allen, Betty Hester and Gloria Marie Warren.

1972 CHAMBER OF COMMERCE BOARD OF DIRECTORS

FRONT: Rudolph Pettersen, Chris Perez, Jack Hoover, Sec. & Treas., Martin E. Parker, Norman G. Whitlow, Fred Bradley. BACK: Robert G. Griffith, Victor Robertson, Jr., Michael E. Grimes, Winfred G. "Wimp" McCoy, President, Virgil Rabb, Jerry Wall, Eugene Quick, Wayne Mann, Vice Pres. Not pictured: Don Hester and Charles Johnson. The Round Rock Chamber of Commerce was chartered in the 1920's with Walter E. Henna as the first president.

ROUND ROCK 4-H CLUB OFFICERS AND LEADERS

This club was organized in 1971 and has 60 members. L to R: Ervin Kaatz, Roxann Kaatz, Ruby Kaatz, Wesley Wigington, Kevin Kaatz, Mitzi Boatright, Mildred Krienke, Pattie Adams and Karl Krienke. President is Wesley Wigington, Vice-President, Roxann Kaatz, Sec. & Treas., Pattie Adams and Reporter Joe Gregory not pictured. Mr. and Mrs. Kaatz and Mr. and Mrs. Krienke are organizational leaders.

Pictured at top is Round Rock's first public School building. Was previously the Southern Presbyterian Institute but became first school in 1883. Was located on college hill where the Col. Todds now live. School burned in 1913.

On left is the new Senior High School which was occupied for classes this year, 1972.

ROUND ROCK PAST PRESIDENTS OF PTA
Founded January, 1918

Mrs. O. M. Bloom	1918-21	Mrs. D. B. Gregg	1952-53
Mrs. Jack Jordan	1921-22	Mrs. H. D. Dollahite	1953-54
Mrs. S. E. Bergstrom	1922-23	Mrs. Leroy Behrens	1954-55
Mrs. W. J. Walsh	1923-24	Dr. & Mrs. J. Cartlidge	1955-56
Mrs. L. W. Ross	1924-25	Mrs. Erwin Bassford	1956-57
Mrs. W. A. Gantt	1925-26	Mr. & Mrs. Weldon Chaffin	1957-58
Mrs. J. T. Hutto	1926-32	Mr. & Mrs. John Bradley	1958-59
Mrs. L. W. Ross	1932-36	Mr. & Mrs. Oscar Bergstrom	1959-60
Mrs. J. Lambert	1936-38	Mr. & Mrs. James McNabb, Jr.	1960-61
Mrs. J. W. Ledbetter	1938-39	Mr. & Mrs. Robert L. Reed	1961-62
Mrs. H. N. Crimm	1939-40	Mr. & Mrs. Robert Burleson	1962-63
Mrs. Eugene Quick	1940-43	Mr. & Mrs. Karl Krienke	1963-64
Mrs. T. G. Wray	1943-45	Mr. & Mrs. Glyn Morsbach	1964-65
Mrs. H. J. Adair	1945-46	Mr. & Mrs. Norman Whitlow	1965-66
Mrs. Leon Behrens	1946-48	Mr. & Mrs. Ray Sanders	1966-67
Mrs. Fred Coffey	1948-50	Mr. and Mrs. Charles Allen	1967-70
Mrs. Oscar Warner	1950-51	Mr. & Mrs. M. J. Cowan	1970-71
Miss Xenia Voigt	1951-52	Mr. & Mrs. Richard C. Baker	1971-72

THE ROUND ROCK P.T.A.

Restored Homes & Buildings

THE NATHAN B. & JUNEBUG SMITH HOME

This home was built in about 1860 and the first known occupants were a Mr. and Mrs. Black. In 1879, Dr. and Mrs. G. T. Cole purchased this house. Dr. Cole was an eye doctor and practiced in this home. Their only child, Mary, married an oilman and they had three children, Georgia Lee, Chester and Quinn, who were reared in the home. The Nathan B. Smith's purchased and restored this home in 1970.

NATHAN B. AND JUNEBUG SMITH WITH DAUGHTER ABIGAIL

"WOODBINE MANSION"

Mr. and Mrs. Andrew J. Nelson were Swedish imigrants who settled in Williamson County in 1854. Prior to his death in 1895, Mr. Nelson established extensive farming enterprises, and served in numerous official capacities with the Swedish Lutheran Church in the town of Round Rock.

It was in 1895 that the newly widowed Mrs. Nelson, with her two sons Thomas Edward and Carl A., started the construction of a very fine residence in Round Rock which took more than four years in the building. The new home was completed and occupied in 1900. After the death of Mrs. Nelson in 1923, the sons continued to live in the mansion while they jointly engaged in numerous commercial and banking ventures.

In 1928, the Nelson brothers encouraged agricultural diversification in Williamson county. They started the first commercial cheese factory in Texas. They provided financing to area farmers who established dairy herds. The cheese factory was purchased by Armour & Co. and continued in production until 1967.

In 1929, T. E. Nelson married and brought his bride, the former Rebecca Young Schofield, to live in the mansion. In 1931, a remodeling was undertaken, which changed the structures facade from victorian to colonial.

The mansion was purchased in 1960 by Mr. and Mrs. Eugene Goodrich. Mrs. Goodrich, the former Jean Lange Crier, Texas artist and antique collector, directed an extensive refurbishing of the structure which was completed in 1968.

Woodbine, in its park like setting, is surrounded by towering elm, pecan, and magnolia trees. The house has eighteen rooms with lofty ceilings, and eight fireplaces. There is a widow's walk on top of the three story structure which commands the view for miles.

Today, the mansion stands as an impressive and rare example of gentle life at the turn of the century.

COLONEL AND MRS. W. N. TODD RESTORED HOME
DOUBLE N ACRES—716 ROUND ROCK AVE.

Colonel and Mrs. W. N. Todd, Jr. moved to Round Rock in 1953 and purchased the old Mexican School which is pictured below. With much work and planning, the Todd home is a lovely place to live and enjoy life.

The Mexican School, which was the original structure of the Todd home, was built by the Texas Relief Commission in 1934.

CORNERSTONE ON TODD HOME
ROUND ROCK SCHOOL-1934
BOARD OF TRUSTEES
Rev. Theo Krienke
Dr. D. B. Gregg
O. L. Brady
A. H. Kaufman
W. J. Walsh
L. W. Ross
Helmer Johnson

STILL BROOK
RESTORED HOME OF
COLONEL AND MRS. A. B. MacNABB

The home on left was built in 1853 or before and was restored in 1953 by the MacNabbs. Original builder unknown, had four rooms with 15 foot ceilings and four fireplaces. Built of native limestone. Was once home of the President of the college.

This home is on Brushy Creek by the round rock for which the town is named.

122

J. A. NELSON BUILDING, BUILT IN 1900

EARLY COMMERCIAL BUILDING
ERECTED TO HOUSE PRIVATE BANK
AS WELL AS HARDWARE AND LUMBER
BUSINESS OF JOHN A. NELSON AND
ASSOCIATES. BANK WAS CLOSED IN
1922; COMMERCIAL USE CONTINUES.
ARCHITECTURALLY IMPORTANT FOR
FACADE OF CAST IRON AND PRESSED
TIN. ORNAMENTED PILASTERS AND
COLUMNS OF THIS TYPE WERE USED
IN MANY LATE 19TH - EARLY 20TH
CENTURY STRUCTURES IN CENTRAL
TEXAS. THIS FRONT IS NOTABLE FOR
ITS CONTINUOUS PRESERVATION. THE
BUILDING IS OF NATIVE LIMESTONE.
RECORDED TEXAS HISTORIC LANDMARK — 1970

Present at unveiling of Historical Marker. L to R: Mayor Dale Hester, Virgial Rabb, E. A. Johnson, Jerry Wall, Russell Koontz, W. G. McCoy, Norman G. Whitlow, Richard C. Baker and James D. Watson.

TOM E. NELSON, JR.

ABOVE: Mrs. John W. Ledbetter, Mrs. D. B. Gregg, Mrs. John Cornforth and Mr. Wayne Bell.
AT RIGHT: Mr. Gus Lundelius, Gus Sager and Oliver Berglund.

THE INN AT BRUSHY CREEK

Built in about 1840 and is registered in National Register in Washington D.C. which makes it a Texas Landmark. Restored in 1969 by Fred Tinnin and Buzz Kelley and now serves as a Historical Country Inn, Serving from a Contintental Menu. Reservations required. Located on IH 35 at The Taylor Exit, Westside, Oldtown, Round Rock, Texas.

YOUTH

BRENT BUSTIN

Above is a typical scene in the dug-out of BRENT BUSTIN MEMORIAL PARK on most any summer evening. This park is located just West of IH 35 next to Old Settlers Park.

THIS PAGE COMPLIMENTS OF BENNIE AND JEAN BUSTIN, PARENTS OF BRENT

1951 ROUND ROCK LITTLE LEAGUE TEAM

Round Rock's first Little League team was organized in 1951 with Mr. Fred Coffe as the organizer and manager with the help of Elmer Cottrell and their wives. Mr. Coffe purchased the uniforms and the equipment was purchased from concession stand sales. The Round Rock Little League became affiliated with the LL in 1952. FRONT: Roy Wolf, Robert Turner, David Killen, James Moore. BACK: Mr. Fred Coffe, Thomas Millegan, Perry Hester, Howard Wolf, Gail Hester, Jerry Miles, Fidenco Zamarippa, Dale Hester, James Adams. Not pictured, Elmer Cottrell, Coach.

COMPLIMENTS OF GAIL HESTER

UNDEFEATED 1971-72 FRESHMAN FOOTBALL TEAM

FIRST ROW: Jerry Cox, Ricky Chipman, Jerry Jones, Charles Wright, Jeff Webb, Greg Futrell, Donnie Hazlewood, Rudy Simmons. SECOND: Edward Able, Ronnie Cox, Darrell Wells, James Anderson, Curtis Edwards, Curtis Reed, Don Joseph, Terry Parker, James Kelly, Mgr. THIRD: Kenneth Palmquist, Kenneth Oryler, Steve Hester, Bruce Snow, Michael Biddy, Doug Sybert, James Thornton, Calvin Griffin, Lawrence Sparks. FOURTH: Glen Bearden, Garland Savage, Clyde Hill, John Carlson, Ronald Moore, James Yancey, Larry Robertson, David Wilkins, Mark Garrett, Coach Buddy Roberts.

1963 ROUND ROCK LITTLE LEAGUE—CHARLES NELSON, COACH
FRONT: Glenn King, Leonard Campbell, Wayne King, Johnny Hood, Bruce Burleson, Tommie Payne.
BACK: Scott Whitlow, Alan Wiley, Steve Gonzales, Larry Madsen, Ronnie Woytek, Skipper Parker and Paul Vernon.

1968 LITTLE LEAGUE TEAM—THE CUBS—UNDEFEATED SEASON
FRONT: Terrence Parker, Bobby Stark, David Cluck, Trenton Jones, Roddy Dill, Teddy Boatright
BACK: Augustine Salinas, Glen Pierce, Harry Mercer, John T. Boatright, Manager, David Wilkins, Michael Biddy and Gary Allemon.

Martha Warren with Fancy Extreme at the 1970 Austin Livestock Show

Nora and Martha Warren with their Grand Champion and Reserve Grand Champion Turkeys at the Austin Show in 1971.

Martha 8 & Nora 5, in 1965. Martha with Outstanding Camper Award, Western Camp.

Martha & Pete—Her FFA project for 1972.

Bob Warren in 1949 with his FFA project of brood sow and litter of pigs.

Nell and Bob Warren proudly look on with Nora Warren and her Reserve Champion Turkey Tom at the 1972 Show.

ROUND ROCK FFA CHAMPIONSHIP BANNERS WON AT 1972 TAYLOR LIVESTOCK SHOW
Osa Corley, Reserve Champion Broilers—Ronnie Cox, Showmanship Award—Bonnie Corley, Championship Broiler Award—Martha Warren with two banners, one for Champion Turkey Hen and one for Champion Turkey Tom—Jim Bingham, Grand Champion Barrow—Steve Hester with his award for the Grand Champion Steer of the show.

Martha Warren with her Champion Turkey Tom at the Taylor Show, 1-21-72

Mr. Earl Seay on the left and Mr. Dennis Templeton

Ronnie Cox in the middle with his prize hog at the 1972 Taylor Livestock Show. Mr. Don Hester and Miss Jane Lester, FFA Sweetheart

THIS PAGE COMPLIMENTS OF MR. AND MRS. BOB WARREN

1972 FUTURE FARMERS OF AMERICA GROUP

FIRST ROW: Dennis Templeton, Advisor, Teddy Boatright, Robert Croker, Darwin Anderson, Alan Robinson, Paul Warner, Treasurer, Bonnie Corley, Secretary, Wesley Wiginton, Sentinel, Mike Seay, President, Ronald Madsen, Vice-Pres., Kevin Kaatz, Reporter, Charley Wright, Robert Currie, Osa Corley, Earl Seay, Advisor. SECOND ROW: Quenton Walden, Robert Mills, John Beltran, Trenton Jones, Kevin Kincaid, Damond Benningfield, Steve Hester, Bobby Stork, Doug Sybert, Stephen Parks, Terrence Parker, Ronnie Cox, Bruce Snow, Wayne Miller, Curtis Reed, Ricky Shipman, Larry Robinson, Robert Madsen. THIRD ROW: Ayron Brooks, Jimmy Townsend, Perry Elam, Ray May, Harold Bingham, Ernest Tanguma, Darwin Herrin, Delbert Holder, David Leppin, Martha Warren, Pat Crouch. FOURTH ROW: Lonnie Ragsdale, Cordell Twomey, Edward Abel, Lupe Ramos, Johnathan Montgomery, Mitzi Boatright, Thomas Holder, Jane Lester, J. W. Huckabay, Jim Bingham, Grady Isaacks, Alvin Woodal, J. T. Cox, Phillip Kitchens, Johnny Boatright, Thomas Isaacks, Phil Frazier, Aaron Springer, Karl Thompson, James Cooper.

Honorable Charles Patterson, State Representative, Speaker at the 1972 FFA Banquet

MISS JANE LESTER

1972
ROUND ROCK FFA SWEETHEART
with her parents

MR. & MRS. CARTER LESTER

SPONSORED BY DOUBLECREEK FARMS, MR. AND MRS. CARTER LESTER, OWNERS.

STEVEN HESTER

GRAND CHAMPION STEER
1972 Taylor Show

Don Hester, father of Steven, in the center,
and FFA Advisor Earl Seay on the left.

SPONSORED BY HESTERS DAIRY KREME, MR. AND MRS. DONALD HESTER, OWNERS

ON LEFT:
1971 Sr. Leadership Team at State Contest. Dennis Templeton, Alan Robinson, Wesley Wiginton, Alvin Woodall, Ronald Madsen, Ray May, Mike Seay, Larry Robinson.

ON RIGHT:
1971 Jr. Leadership Team at District Contest. Charley Wright, Osa Corley, Martha Warren, Robert Currie, Bobby Stork, Ronnie Cox, Doug Sybert, Edward Abel, Pat Crouch, Lonnie Ragsdale, Earl Seay, Advisor.

PICTURED LOWER LEFT
FFA Fishing Trip to Lake Sam Rayburn, Summer of 1971

Dennis Templeton—kneeling, Travis Gage, Ronald Madsen, Mike Seay, John Beltran, Earl Seay, Richard Ekvall, Wesley Wiginton, not pictured, Arnold Peterson.

PICTURED LOWER RIGHT

FFA at A&M Veterinary School
FRONT: Dennis Templeton, Adv., Darwin Anderson, Osa Corley
MIDDLE: Alan Robinson, Lonnie Ragsdale, Charley Wright, Martha Warren, Bonnie Corley.
BACK: Stephen Parks, John Beltran, Damon Benningfield, Jane Lester, Wesley Wiginton, Ray May, Earl Seay, Advisor.

1972 HONORARY FFA MEMBERS
Mr. Bobby Warren
Mrs. Wanda Carlson

ABOVE

BONNIE CORLEY with Champion Lamb at the 1971 Georgetown
Fat Stock Show.

ABOVE

OSA CORLEY with Reserve Champion Broilers at the 1972 Taylor
Fat Stock Show. Lane Lester, FFA Sweetheart.

****

****

BELOW

BONNIE CORLEY with Champion Broilers at the 1972 Taylor
Show. Jane Lester FFA Sweetheart.

BELOW

JIM BINGHAM with Grand Champion Barrow at the 1972 Taylor
Show. Jane Lester and N. G. Whitlow.

THIS PAGE COMPLIMENTS OF MR. AND MRS. OSA F. CORLEY

POP WARNER RAMS
PEE WEE TEAM 1971

MANAGERS
Sonny Balch
Ron Morrison
Eddie Breaux

SPONSORS
ROUND ROCK LIONS CLUB
HOLDER PLUMBING
BRUSHY CREEK BUILDERS

FRONT: Jerry Baskett, Danny Balch, Robert Herrera, Bobby LeClair, Clay Schumann, James Beauchamp, Jimmy Holder, Jeff Wagner. MIDDLE: Bubba Toungate, David DeLaCruz, Fabian Ramos, James Patcheske, Gilbert Beltran, Allen Schumann, Wade Kitts. TOP: Ronnie Wall, Terry Roberts, Greg Fielder, Von Breaux, Monte Eckert, Ron Sanders, Glen Behrens.

1971 POP WARNER TEAM
FRONT: Patrick Torres, Kenneth Holder, Gary Giebel, Buddy Poncik, Eddie Ishmael, Glen Watson, William Simons, Chris Perez. MIDDLE: Thomas Moreland, Chris Earl, James Holder, Kevin Johnson, Michael Snow, Ronald, Rudy DeLaRosa. TOP: Mike Grimes, Todd Hawthorne, Mark Remmert, Carter Hill, Jeffery Hudgins, Doug Remmert, J. Hollier.

1971 RAM
CHEERLEADERS

Tammy Roberts
Debra Balch
Charisse Fite
Jan Cowan
Delane Watson

Mary Ann Baskett
Carolyn Holder
Diane Schumann
Linda Holder
Geneva Fielder

Local Business

ADAMS SERVICE STATION
W. F. "Bub" Adams and son George Adams in front of station at 508 North Mays Street.

ANDERSON AUTO REPAIR
Brady "Red" Anderson on right with helper Pete Castillo in garage at 406 N. Lee St.

AUSTIN AMERICAN–STATESMAN

Pictured above is Derryl Swinden and Jack Swinden, the "paperboys" for Round Rock as they roll papers for an afternoon delivery. The Swinden boys "throw" both the morning and the afternoon papers. They have thrown the Austin American Statesman for two years. They are awakened by their parents Mr. and Mrs. C. J. Swinden each morning at 1:30am to roll and throw some 305 papers and some 500 papers on Sunday morning plus putting papers in their paper racks. In the afternoons, Derryl and Jack roll and throw 160 papers. The afternoon papers are usually thrown between 2:10 and 4:45pm.

BEHRENS DITCHING SERVICE

William Adolph "Boo" Behrens with some of his equipment. Specializing in back-hoe and ditching work and septic tanks.

BEHRENS BEAUTY SHOPPE

Pictured on left is Round Rock's first beauty shop in 1930. This shop was then the McCann Beauty Shoppe and was located on the site where the Central Elementary School is now located. The Beauty Shop was in the front room of the home. Her son, Jack McCann, also worked in the business and received his license in 1935.

The Behrens Beauty Shoppe is now located at 408 North Georgetown Street and is still in operation after 42 years service.

BENNINGFIELD AUTOMOTIVE SERVICE
L to R: John Bergstrom, Pete Correa, Vale Benningfield, Owner, Damon Benningfield.

BO-KAY FLORIST
Susie Ramos, on left, Ruth Bernard and son Michael and David Bernard, the owners.

Tommy Moore and Weldon L. Tredemeyer with antique automobiles.

BIG "T" PACKAGE STORE

Everyday special------------Courtesy and Service

RUN IN before you RUN OUT

Gag Novelties . . . . Gifts . . . . Imported Wines

Bar Supplies . . . . . . Crushed Ice

Glassware

Tommy Moore, Owner

BRUSHY CREEK PROPERTIES
Complete Real Estate Service

EDWARD D. QUICK

JAMES W. CAROTHERS

BURK'S MOBIL SERVICE
"Your Business is appreciated"—Edwin A. "Eddie" Burk and L. P. "Bud" Parker

CASTILLO TEXACO

Luz Castillo, Jr. with Javier Hernandez at the pumps of Castillo's Station at 600 W. Anderson. Intersection of IH 35, Round Rock Ave, W. Anderson and N. Lee St.

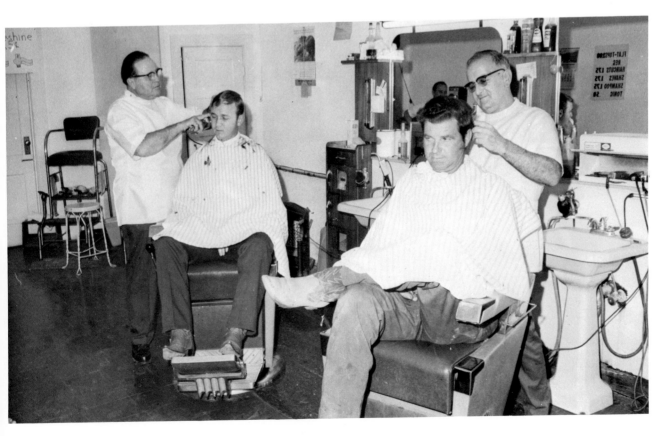

CITY BARBER SHOP

Located at 106 E. Main and owned and operated by Mr. Sam Kerns. Mr. Kerns is cutting Mike Giles hair in back chair and Winfred Novak has Sammy Jackson in front chair.

CANYON CONSTRUCTION COMPANY
On Quick Hill Road

WAYNE E. LOTT, OWNER
L to R: Patty Schilling, Joe Blaylock and Linda Feduniak

Col. George J. Callon (USAF Ret.), Ex-fighter pilot retired to this interesting business of woodworking and antique refinishing after 27 years in the Air Force. His woodwork shop is in Old Round Rock at 18 Old Chisholm Trail.

CLARICE'S TAVERN
Owned and operated by Mrs. Clarice DeBack—Serving Bar-B-Q, Sausage, Chili, Burgers

COLONIAL ACRES RETIREMENT & NURSING HOME
Located at 301 West Taylor Ave. One of Round Rock's fine retirement homes.

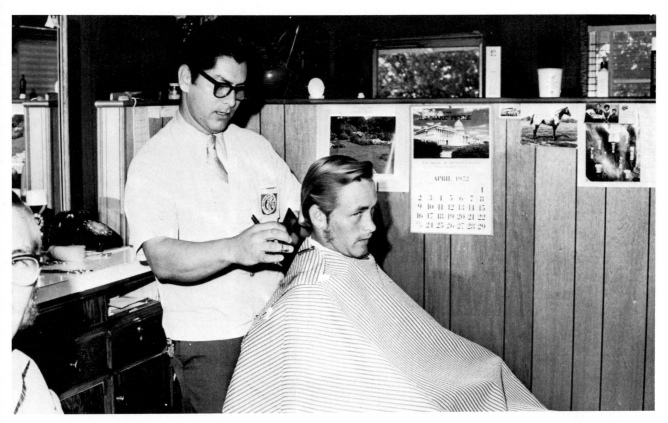

CHRIS' HAIR STYLES FOR MEN

Hair Styling and Regular Cuts   Located on Sam Bass Road in Old Town.

LINDA'S BEAUTY SHOP
Located on Sam Bass Road in Old Town. Linda Perez is owner and operator. Chris and Linda are husband and wife team. L. To R.: Rosemary Perez, Linda Perez, Owner, Darlene Lackey and Sue Boyd, with Mrs. Ruby Bradley in the chair.

Paul Jones; Charles Sartor, MGR; Kenneth Balusek.

The Condra Funeral Home, which is located at Main and Harris Streets in Round Rock, Began operation in May of 1947. The home was first managed by Paul J. Groody and later by Jack Hightower. Mr. Charles Sartor and his family came to Round Rock in 1954 and he assumed the management of the funeral home. The Chapel facilities were fully remodeled in 1965; having a seating capacity of 180, and a private family room with a seating of another 50. The funeral home is a branch office of the Condra Funeral Home of Taylor. The firm is a member of the National Selected Morticians.

DOUBLECREEK FARM, INC.

A Day Camp, Private First Grade & Kindergarten. Owned and operated by Carter & Trudy Lester. In front of school is Wesley Wigington, Bruce Kirtley, Jane Lester on "Sparkplug," Trudy Lester, Carter Lester and Paul Warner. Provides swimming, Horseback riding and outdoor activities for boys and girls ages 4-14. On Gattis School Rd.

FRONTIER FOODS

A Friendly Place to Trade Owned and operated by Mr. and Mrs. Wayne Mann. In front of store at 117 East Main St.: Charlie Anderson, Joyce Pugh, Eddie Gaitan, Pete Comacho, Jackie Mann and Wayne Mann, the owners.

FARMERS' STATE BANK BOARD OF DIRECTORS

M. J. Cowan, Perry Mayfield, Virgil Rabb, Tom E. Nelson, Jr., Richard C. Baker and Norman G. Whitlow. Not pictured is G. R. Lundelius and Russell Koontz.

"Offering A Courteous, Efficient Service To Williamson County Since 1920"

A BETTER PLACE TO BANK   LOCATED 205 EAST MAIN STREET

MEMBER FDIC

OFFICERS AND EMPLOYEES OF FARMERS' STATE BANK

FRONT: Nydia Vallejo, Linda Orn, Jo Ann Henna, Mary Olson, Joe Perez, R. E. McMinn.
MIDDLE: Donna Sanders, Mary Burklund, Margie Prinz, Norma Bearden, Mozelle Nicks, Ann Houseton, Clarice Hanstrom, Barbara McCasland.
BACK: Ron Morrison, Bernice Remmert, Judy Creek, Russell Koontz, Tom E. Nelson, Jr., M. J. Cowan and N. G. Whitlow

FIRST
NATIONAL
BANK
OF ROUND ROCK

(In Organization*)

*Preliminary Approval Granted By Comptroller Of The Currency On June 1, 1972

HENDERSONS
School Supplies—Clothing—Piece Goods—Hardware—Small Appliances
Mrs. Ima Lentz, Manager, in the middle, Mildred Powell on left and Josephine May.

E. H. JOHNSON FEED AND PAINT CENTER
Located at 108 East Main Street. Owned and operated by Mr. and Mrs. E. H. Johnson.

HESTER'S DAIRY KREME
Don and Betty Hester, Owners. Located at 409 Round Rock Ave. L-R: Don Hester, Steve Hester, Shelley Hester, Mildred Townsend, Mary Guzman, Clifford Hickman, Betty Pierce, Becky Derrick, Deborah Gavit, Mike Davis, Sylvia Hernandez, Robin Hester, Jeff Hester and Mrs. Betty Hester.

HESTER'S ARCO SERVICE STATION
Automotive Repair, Used Cars, Motor Vehicle Inspection, Tuneups, Brakes, Tires
Dwight Hardin, Henry Nava and owner Gail Hester stand in front of station

Round Rock Insurance

Deison Associates - Jordan Ins. Agency

J. J. Hoover—agent
John Jordan—agent

Pictured left to right
Holly Hoover, John Jordan,
J. J. Hoover, Charlotte Sautter,
Sue Hoover

M. O. Deison Insurance Agency—Founded 1926 by Murry Deison
pictured above: Murry Deison & Mrs. Deison

John M. Jordan Insurance Agency—Established 1916
Operated From 1935 on by John M. Jordan—
pictured: Mr. Jordan receiving 25 yrs. award from T. R. Mansfield, Pres./Gulf Ins. Co.

JOHNSON TEXACO
Road Service—Minor Repairs—Brakes—Wheel Balancing—Tires—Batteries—111 N. Mays St.
Charles Johnson, Owner, Jimmy Heller & Michael Marx.

JOYCE ROBERTS TWIRLING AND DANCING STUDIO
Pictured above: Audrie Daniels, Kathy Krienke, Brenda Traugott, Joan Zimmerman,
Pattie Armstrong, Janet Traugott and Joyce Roberts.

On Right: Tammy Roberts with trophy for National Six Year Old Twirler. She was
Texas Solo Champion and first Little Miss Round Rock.

ROY A. KRIENKE

CONTRACTOR

BACK-HOE
EXCAVATING
UTILITIES

Box 276
Round Rock, Texas
78664

LaBELLA SALON OF BEAUTY
Complete Beauty Care—Individually Created Coiffures and Shaping—Tinting—Frosting
Mrs. Vincent Sanchez, Owner   109 West Main Street

LARSON SUPPLY COMPANY
Lyman S. Larson, Owner
Wholesale Automotive Supplies—Your Wagon Jobber—202 Sunset Drive—Ph. 255-3510

LUPE'S GULF STATION
"A Service Station—Not A Filling Station"—Minor Auto Repairs—Wash—Polish—Lube—Tires—Batteries—Cars Picked Up & Delivered. ABOVE
Lupe and Robert Madrigal on driveway.

LEIGH MOTORS FORD—MACK LEIGH AND H. R. LEIGH, OWNERS

Charles Gresham, Charles Watt, Don Hoyle, Ernest Johnson, Ralph Granzin, L. Klepac.

Bill Conely, Jerry Fergurson
Tom Fears, Sales Mgr.

Brenda Fuetner, Mack Leigh, Jr.
Glenda Morrison, Bookkeeper

GONZALO MEDEL in front of his barber shop on South Mays Street. This was the first licensed Latin barber shop in Round Rock. BOTTOM: Medel in front of his tavern.

THE PERRY MAYFIELD RANCH. Located just west of Round Rock is "home" for Perry Mayfield with his herds of cattle. Pictured above is Perry and brother Dick as they pen up some 100 cows with calves. Beautiful oaks, good grass and rolling hills with plenty of deer, make up this choice ranch.

Bottom picture shows the chute that Perry Mayfield shipped over $500,000.00 feeder cattle yearly for several years. Chute was used over 40 years. Standing with Perry Mayfield in center is Dick Mayfield on right and Martin E. Parker on the left.

MAC'S DRIVE-IN GROCERY
Located South of Round Rock on IH 35 next to Stuckey's. Owned and operated by Mr. and Mrs. W. E. McCarty. Mr. Johnny Sanford, Mgr. above in front of store.

MID-TEX FARM SUPPLY & CO-OP
Fertilizers—Feeds—Seed—Hardware—Tires—Oil—Batteries and all needs for the farmer. Mr. H. H. McKenzie and Mrs. Allene McKenzie, Managers with Lawrence E. Scott.

DR. ROY J. MOORE, CHIROPRACTOR
206 East Main Street

Spinal Analysis—X-Ray

Across from the Farmers State Bank

MORSE GROCERY & STATION

Mr. and Mrs. S. J. "Red" Morse, Owners

Located on F. M. 1325

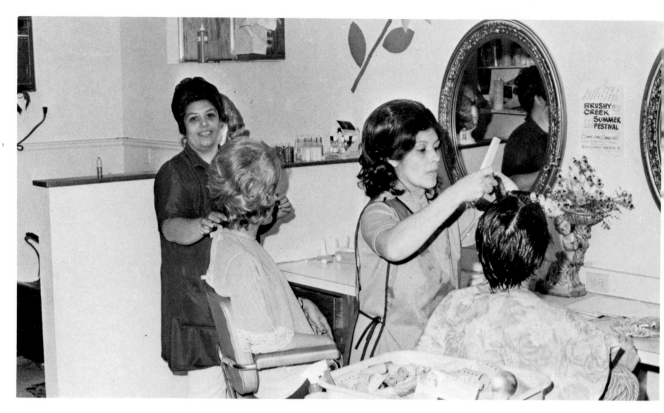

OLIVIA'S SALONS

"There is no substitute for professional hair care"—Hair Goods and Services. Olivia Castillo, Owner on left, with Barbara Childers in chair and Mrs. Mary Carlin at work on the right. Olivia's of Round Rock at 411 N. Lampasas Street.

PETTERSEN GROCERY & MARKET

Mrs. Annie Bustin, Elmer Hester, Sherrod Prewitt, Eddie Gaitan, Pete Commacho and Mr. Rudolph Pettersen, Operator and Owner of store at 117 E. Main from 1946 until 1971. The store was formerly operated by Hoyt Crimm. Present Owner, Mr. Wayne Mann.

QUICK PHARMACY

Owned and operated by Mr. Eugene O. Quick at 204 East Mains Street since 1942. Employees L-R: Linda Townsend, Mary Jane Wolf, Ebba Quick, Joyce Swindall, Eugene O. Quick, Owner, Agnes Quick, Lydia Wolf, Elsie Wolf, Norma Ekvall, Valorie Carothers.

THE ECONOMY DRUG STORE

Inside same building in 1915. Mr. Green Noble was the owner. Same fixtures still used.

VIC ROBERTSON GROCERY
ONE STOP SERVICE   210 N. MAYS   OPEN 7 DAYS A WEEK

Vic Robertson, Jr., Owner, with Ernest Lee Daniel

ROBERTSON'S FABRICS

This is a 3rd generation store located at 101 E. Main Street, the same building of Sam Bass's last gun fight. The gun battle began inside this building. The Robertson family has been in business nearly 100 years in Round Rock.

In the picture below, interior of the modern store today with Lucy Carlin, Amanda Carlin and Dora and John D. Robertson, Sr., the owners.

HARRY ROBERTSON INSURANCE & REAL ESTATE
109 South Mays
In Business Since 1953

ROBINSON AUTO SERVICE
100 East Main St.
Motor Overhauls—Tuneups—Brake Service—Mufflers—Tailpipes—Wheel Balancing
Mr. J. D. Robinson, Owner with over 15 years experience and Louie Wilson.

ROUND ROCK AUTO SUPPLY
Auto Parts & Supplies—Quality Name Brands—Good Stocks and Selections
Harry Haynes, Owner, with son Craig Haynes and Leslie Madsen—119 East Main Street.

ROUND ROCK BUILDING MATERIALS
Hardware—Paints—Insulation—Shingles & Wallboard—Cement—Plastic Pipe—Wallpaper
James G. Peters, Owner, on left, with Durwood Bourland. Located at 111 West Main St.

ROUND ROCK LIME COMPANY
In operation for over a century
OFFICE STAFF: Van Davison, Dorthy Tomancak, Stewart Dahlin, Carol Felts, Fayrene Zimmerman, Mavinee Bredthauer, Clara Carter.

ROUND ROCK ELECTRIC COMPANY
Residential—Commercial—Industrial—Contracting and Repairs
Lenny Hedrick, Owner   Jerry Crain, Assistant

ROUND ROCK CHILD DEVELOPMENT CENTER. Ruth Burleson is Project Director of Head Start. Burma Dean Gaddison, on left in top is Director, Terry DeLaCruz and Thelma Woods.
Lower picture above, Mrs. Nancy Mays and Teresa Carlin work with the children.

RUBIO'S GROCERY
Complete Meat Market—Fruits—Vegetables—Located at 107 West Main Street.
MACK & LORENZO RUBIO, OWNERS   Open 7 days a week.

BILLY HENNA, OWNER

L to R: Virgil McCasland, Lester Staton, David McCasland, Mike Davis, Willie Hurd, Stanford Gibbs, Charles Staton, Lucky Coupland, Charles Foster, Jimmy Pate.

ROUND ROCK MOTOR COMPANY
"NO STUTTERING WE TRADE"   416 N. MAYS   TEN MINUTES FROM AUSTIN

ROUND ROCK TRADING MART
Used Furniture—Used Clothing   110 S. Mays   Old Books—Collector's Items
"A little bit of everything"
"IN BEAUTIFUL DOWNTOWN ROUND ROCK"
MR. AND MRS. L. J. ROBINSON, OWNERS

Left to right: Tony Connell, Larry Robinson, and L. J. "Spike" Robinson, Owner

MY,

Telephone service has come a long way since the early 1900's when all subscribers had crank-type telephones and the voice with a smile was a local girl who knew everyone's telephone number.

Service was the watchword in those days and still is with Southwestern Bell. Modern telephones, one-plus dialing and sophisticated switching equipment which can speed your calls across town or across the nation are a part of today's modern telephone service. We've changed because Round Rock has changed—and our goal is to keep up with progress in this thriving community.

HOW YOU'VE CHANGED!

Mamie Gray (now Mrs. Mamie Biel) became a telephone operator in 1913 and knew the number of every subscriber in town. She was on duty the evening of November 11, 1918 when a telephone call from Austin announced the signing of the Armistice that ended World War I.

The telephone had become less of a luxury and more of a necessity in Round Rock when Ora Dettenhaim served here as Chief Operator during the 1930's.

When dial service came to Round Rock October 27, 1951, telephone people Fred Fullerton, Alex Gordon, W. D. Graves, Mrs. Roy Ross and Mrs. Betsy Nehring posed for one last picture around the "number, please" switchboard which was replaced by the automatic dial equipment.

Southwestern Bell

173

STUCKEY'S PECAN SHOPPE
Mr. and Mrs. W. C. Hines, Managers

Located just south of Round Rock on IH 35, this store offers a place to stop and relax for weary travelers. Standing in front of the store L to R: W. C. Hines, Minnie Hines, Denise Dearing, Willene Gage, Carl Burklund, Lucinda Walther, Becky Nees, Mike Cummings. PICTURED BELOW: Mr. and Mrs. W. C. Hines, the Managers, proudly look over their store.

SAM BASS STEAK HOUSE
A. W. Charpiot, Owner

Three Private Dining Rooms—One Room Seats 340 People—Located IH 35 and 79 East.
Private Parties

SAM BASS STEAKHOUSE PERSONNEL
Carol Williamson, Shirley Charpiot, Eva Easoz, Estelle Kirk, Maxine Charpiot and A. W. Charpiot, Owners.

TEXAS
POWER & LIGHT
CO.
Robert Bairrington, Serviceman
Beth Carlile, Office Clerk & Cashier.
W. G. McCoy, Local Manager
TEXAS POWER & LIGHT COMPANY has been
in this same office since 1927.

Pictured below: TEXAS POWER AND LIGHT
COMPANY line crew prepares to erect a pole in a
city park on Brushy Creek.

THE FLINT SHOP
The Davie Boultinghouse family: DAVIE, FRANCES, DEBRA & CHRIS—In handmade buckskins.

Davie started building muzzle loading rifles as a hobby some 5 years ago. He has now developed it into a full time profession. The rifles are hand crafted from the finest materials available, not only for beauty, but for the superb accuracy required for competition shooting. The entire family travels to several other states and all over Texas each year to test their skill against other shooters. Davie and Frances have both won the Texas State Championship in the past and the family has collected 225 trophies and ribbons in the past 5 years at different matches. Davie and Frances both graduated from Round Rock High School. Davie cuts flints which fires the flintlock rifles, hence the name, The Flint Shop. His flints are used by shooters all over the U.S.A. He also makes beautiful hunting knives from tool steel and uses deer antlers for handles. The knives also are used all over the U.S.A. and as far away as New Zealand. Davie specializes in muzzle loading rifles and pistols only. The beauty and craftmanship of these guns must be seen to fully appreciate them. The Boultinghouse family plans to have a complete muzzle loading gun shop in the near future. The present shop is located at Route 1, Box 116-A, Round Rock, Texas.

TOMANET CORPORATION
Shirley Jackson, Secretary and Dwight Lamb, Vice-President. 109 East Main Street.

LUM C. TOUNGATE ARCO SERVICE STATION
Located at 409 West Taylor, IH 35 & Highway 79. In the middle of a growing town. Mr. Lum Toungate stands on the drive with his three sons Larry, Craig and Jimmy.

THE U. S. POST OFFICE EMPLOYEES

FRONT: Clyde Dannelley, Conrad E. Zimmerman, Martin E. Parker, Postmaster, and Karl Krienke. BACK: Robert C. Foxworth, Richard Barber, J. M. Archer, Milton T. Krienke, Theodore J. Zimmerman, Jr., and Harry Noren.

The Round Rock Post Office is a very old post office. The records in the National Archives in Washington D.C. show that the first post office was established May 27, 1851 as Brushy. Its name was changed to Round Rock on August 24, 1854.
Listed below are names of all Round Rock Postmasters and the dates of appointments.

Thomas C. Oatts	5-27-1851	Mrs. Kate F. Martin	11-20-1885
Robert J. Hill	6-11-1860	Edward E. Diggs	6-17-1889
George W. Davis	11-28-1860	Joseph H. Holt	5-10-1893
Miss Jordana A. Davis	12-27-1865	Robert R. Hyland	6-19-1897
G. W. Davis	10-11-1886	John A. Hyland	7-29-1911
John Rowland	1-5-1867	Steve B. Wright	1-5-1916
Finas A. Stone	12-9-1874	Merrell M. Jester	9-1-1919
August B. Palm	10-30-1876	Frank L. Aten	2-10-1922
Holman T. Ham	12-5-1877	John W. Ledbetter	1-8-1932
August B. Palm	12-26-1877	Robert E. Johnson	3-31-1943
Joseph J. Boone	9-6-1880	Martin E. Parker	12-29-1965
John T. Haynes	5-20-1881		

The postmaster's salary in 1853 was $20.34 annually and the Post Office's proceeds in 1853 were $23.02. The Round Rock Post Office changed from 4th class to 3rd class in 1902. The Post Office moved from the Masonic Building, which was built in 1878, to the present location at 211 East Main Street, in 1960.

The first official postal service in the USA—1639, Benjamin Franklin was First Postmaster General in 1775, First registered mail—1855, Pony Express—1860, Rural Delivery—1896, Airmail—1918. Letter rate in 1933-3 cents, 1959-4 cents, 1963-5 cents, 1968-6 cents, 1971-8 cents. The U.S. Post Office Department became U.S. Postal Service on July 1, 1971.

TRINITY LUTHERAN HOME

ABOVE: Trinity Lutheran Home entrance on East Main Street. Built on site of Trinity Lutheran College founded in 1904. This million dollar extension was built in 1969. Trinity Lutheran Home has 100 residents and is staffed with 75 to 80 workers.

ABOVE: Mrs. La Verne Reinhardt Administrator, Trinity Lutheran Home in 1972.

RIGHT: Pastor Robert E. Fellows, former Administrator of home, Mrs. D. B. Gregg, center, and Mrs. J. W. Ledbetter as Official Texas Historical Marker was unveiled to dedicate Trinity Lutheran College on May 28, 1972. Mrs. Gregg and Mrs. Ledbetter are members of Historical Committee.

WAG-A-BAG GROCERY

Located at 701 East Taylor. Wag-A-Bag carries complete line of groceries, picnic supplies, beer and ice. Open 7 days a week. 6:30 A.M. 'till 10 P.M.

L to R: Virgil S. Rabb, Owner, Coy Benningfield, Mrs. Travis Lann, Mrs. Leola Gersbock and Mrs. Johnnie C. Roepke.

WESTINGHOUSE ELECTRIC CORPORATION

A new addition to the Round Rock community is the multi-million dollar Gas Turbine Systems Plant now being constructed by the Westinghouse Electric Corporation.

Located on a 200 acre site on Interstate 35, the Plant will employ over 700 people at full operation. The turbines manufactured here will provide electricity for cities around the globe.

The plant's specially designed, direct computer controlled machines will give Round Rock the world's most modern, heavy machining gas turbine facility.

The attractive facility is designed to eliminate air, noise, and water polution. Planned with features to enhance the working environment, the plant will include a spacious and modernistic People Court. Covered by an Astrodome-like, transparent roof, the enclosed patio area will be visible from the manufacturing floor.

Heading the Westinghouse Central Texas operation is Plant Manager Don J. Leonard. A 20-year veteran with Westinghouse, Mr. Leonard joins the new plant from the company's Marine Division at Sunnyvale, California.

DONALD J. LEONARD

Manager
Austin Gas Turbine Plant
Westinghouse Electric Corporation

CONSTRUCTION 1972—WESTINGHOUSE BUILDS IN ROUND ROCK

THE TINY TOT NURSERY

Owned and operated by Mrs. Carroll Hardin at 201 Vista Drive. FRONT: Christine Carlin, Todd Grelle, Amy Milliam, Candy Pinson, Mike McMaster, Cindy DeLeon, Joey Johnson. SECOND: Kelley Kovar, Russell Loeve, Milesa Toungate, Freddie Henry, Ray Laffery, Danna King, Drake Shirley, Jeanette Jaecks, James Valdez. THIRD: Mrs. Carroll Hardin, Tommy Milliam, Sharron Jackson, Bobby Boyd, Kathy Crislip, Robin Heisch, Dare Lovett, Kevin Reinhardt, Mary Mireles. BACK: Dana Toungate, Darrell Toungate, Kim Henry, Michelle Cody and Lisa Sincik.

JERRY WALL ASSOCIATES

REAL ESTATE AND BUILDERS LOCATED AT 109 WEST TAYLOR

Jerry Wall and Glenda Wall, seated. Standing: Nell Free, Ed Cain, Jean Arnold, John Matthews, Linda Boyd and Nancy Stried.

WALSH TELEVISION & APPLIANCES
103 East Main
Television—Refrigerators—Freezers—Air Conditioners—Home Laundries

WHITE AUTO STORE
110 East Main

THE HOME OF GREATER VALUES
Mr. and Mrs. Elwin Hudson
Owners and Operators

Every day low prices on
Refrigerators and Freezers
Washing Machines & Dryers
Sporting Goods—Toys—Radios
Televisions—Heaters—Ranges
Air Conditioners
Bicycles—Fishing Tackle
Garden Supplies & Tools
Parts & Supplies
Lawn Mowers

WHITE CROWN CAMPERS MFG. CO.
Located at 724 Round Rock Ave., builders of custom built campers and production models.
Boyce Langley, Dean White, Jr., Dean White, Sr., the owner and John Campbell

WOYTEK INSURANCE AGENCY
211 Round Rock Avenue

Mr. Ray Woytek and Mrs. Ella Mae Woytek

Agent Farmers Insurance Group

THEO ZIMMERMAN PUMPS SALES & SERVICE
Water Storage Tanks—Windmills—State Licensed Master Plumber—Water System Service.

Theo Zimmerman and wife Maudie, owners and operators with Joan and Chris in front of their business at 104 S. Lampasas. Arthur Grosskopf, Larry Boyd and Bernie Barnes help in the business. Mr. and Mrs. Zimmerman purchased the business from O. A. Voigt in 1947. This is one of the oldest businesses in Round Rock. Mr. Voigt opened his own business about 1910 in the building shown in the picture on lower left. This picture made about 1928 shows the business where the city hall is now located. Later the business was moved to 119 E. Main. Mr. Emil Zimmerman, father of Theo Zimmerman, is shown on lower right. He was employed with O. A. Voigt from 1920 until 1958.

1923 Ford   1972 Picture

Fred M. and Ester Anderson in 1923 with a new Model "T" Ford and as they are today in their home at 204 North Stone. They have 4 children; Inez, Moody, Joe D., and Franklin.

ERNEST R. AND MANCY ANDERSON
210 San Saba Street

Mr. and Mrs. Ernest R. Anderson lived on a farm just south of Round Rock for many years until retirement. Mr. Anderson delivered milk in Round Rock for several years. Pictured below is the Ernest and Mancy Anderson Family taken on their 50th wedding anniversary. They were married November 7, 1916. L. to R.: Ernest and Mancy Anderson, Dudley and Laura Homeyer, Wilbur and Thelma Munson, Ernest Nelson and Gladys Johnson.

THE EUGENE O. BECK FAMILY

The Eugene Becks live on a ranch west of Round Rock on Ranch Road 620. The Becks have lived in the Round Rock area most of their life. Standing in their home above: Mr. Eugene Beck, Regan, Mrs. Genelle Beck, Kay Lynn and Jan in front. Pictured below is Eugene on his horse as he goes out to round up some of his livestock.

MR. AND MRS. OSCAR T. BENGTSON, SR.

The Oscar T. Bengtson's have one son, Oscar T. Bengtson, Jr. and one daughter, Mrs. Robert (Carol) Champion, Jr. Mrs. Bengtson was the former Ruth Carlson.

MR. AND MRS. OSCAR T. BENGTSON, JR.

Oscar T. "Teddy" and Carolyn with Mark, live at 101 Bellaire Circle. Carolyn was the former Carolyn Carlson.

THE ROBERT H. BEHRENS FAMILY—Steven, Robert H., Glenn, Joylene and Randy

THE BEHRENS BOYS—Kelley, Steven, Glenn, Brian, Randy and Willy

THE WILLIAM ADOLPH BEHRENS FAMILY—William A., Willy and Bess

FAMILY OF OSIE M. AND EMMA LOU CRAIN

LEFT: Children: Gaylen, Randel Joe, Jerra, Linda

MIDDLE LEFT: Gaylen and Diann. Their children: Kelly and Chadwick.

MIDDLE RIGHT: Jerra and Merry with Cassie.

LOWER LEFT: Randel Joe and Betty Sue. Their children: Jason, Jon, Susan Elizabeth.

LOWER RIGHT: Joel and Linda Hargis.

THE DAVID CARLIN, SR. FAMILY

FRONT: Theresa, Molly, David Carlin, Sr., Refugia Carlin, Mary, and Lucy.
BACK: James, Janie, David L., Carlos, Robert, Ruben, Ermalinda, and Rudolph. Mr. David Carlin, Sr. has lived his entire life in Round Rock. He married his wife Refugia in 1940 and have reared their 12 children near St. Williams Church.

MARY AND DAVID L. CARLIN
AND CHRISTINA

JANIE AND CONCEPTION CASTILLO
WITH MARCO AND ANNA MARIE

193

THE WALTER (BOXY) ELAM FAMILY

FRONT: Zane and Evon. BACK: Elaine, Loreha (Cricket), Walter (Boxy), Perry, Lucy.

A 1953 picture taken in front of the Sam Bass Cafe on Main Street, Round Rock. Boxy holding Lucy, Cricket and Elaine.

194

Walter (Boxy) Elam in his U.S. Navy uniform. Taken during WW II in 1942.

THE ROLAND HELGE FAMILY

W. R. Helge, Avenell Perry, Jr., Roland Helge, Tirie Helge, Orlena Self, Travis Helge.

LOWER PICTURE. FRONT: Micheal Self, Orlena Self, Roland Helge, Tirie Helge, Avenell Perry, Jr., Stephen Jackson. MIDDLE: Russell Helge, Carol Helge, Scott Jackson. BACK: Sheryl Self, Bobby Self, W. R. Helge, Travis Helge, Linda Helge, Edward Perry, Jr., Nitagail Jackson.

JOHN N. & BERTHA S. JOHNSON ON HONEYMOON IN JANUARY 1921

ON LEFT: In front, John N. & Bertha Johnson. In Back: Ernest Nelson Johnson, John Bruce Johnson and Bertha Marie Johnson Keller. Picture made in December of 1962.

LOWER LEFT: Grandchildren and great grandchildren of the J. N. Johnsons. Ann, Nelson, Jayne, Harvey, Nanette, Johnny, Jay, Kevin, Pamela, Kolm, Kerry Leigh.

ON RIGHT: John Bruce Johnson holds turnips grown on J. N. Johnson vegetable farm 3 miles east of Round Rock in 1943.

These four turnips weighed 24 pounds.

THE ERVIN A. KAATZ RANCH

The Ervin A. Kaatz ranch is located approximately one mile from the city limits of Round Rock on Highway 79. It has Highway 79 as its frontage and Brushy Creek running through the back of it.

Ervin and his wife Ruby were both born and reared in Williamson County on farms in the Thrall and New Bern area. Ervin went to the Army January 3, 1940 and married Ruby Petzolt in 1944. He served in WW II and received a Battlefield Commission in the Infantry while in the European Theatre. He was retired and permanently incapacitated in 1948 from World War II service.

Ervin and Ruby have five children, four sons and one daughter. Ervin Jr., Roger, Kevin, Roxann and Shannon. The Kaatz family moved to the E.A.K. Ranch in 1960 after living in Austin since 1948, where Mr. Kaatz is in the automobile business.

The E.A.K. Ranch for its main enterprise breeds registered quarter horses and has had most of the time as many as twenty brood mares and a stallion. But in recent years, the breeding program has been cut down with strictly quality in production in mind; mares such as Marilyn Twist and Scoot Reeda King. The ranch also has cattle from time to time.

The Kaatz family are members of the Palm Valley Lutheran Church, The American Quarter Horse Association, Central Texas Cutting Horse Association, The National Cutting Horse Association, Williamson County Cattleman's Association, Life members of Angus Assn., Williamson County Sheriff's Posse, The Farm Bureau, Austin Junior Chamber of Commerce and the 4-H Club. Mr. Kaatz was state Vice President of the 1955 and 1956 Jaycees. He is also Vice President of the Austin Livestock Show Committee as manager of the Registered Quarter Horse show.

The Kaatz family loves the Round Rock area. The children especially love the Round Rock School. Ervin Jr. received his degree in Animal Science from Texas A&M and is now assistant County Agent of Montgomery County at Conroe. Roger has just finished his first year at Tarlton State College. The other three children are still in school at Round Rock.

THE JOHN W. LEDBETTER FAMILY

The John W. Ledbetter family was one of the early pioneer families who settled in Old Round Rock. Descendants of this family have lived in Round Rock since their early settlement here.

ABOVE: Mrs. John W. Ledbetter, Sr. on left, Mrs. James (Nan) Antill, Mr. James Antill and their daughters Gena Kathryn and Bernice Anne.

THE JOHN W. LEDBETTER, JR. FAMILY

Mr. John W. Ledbetter, Jr., John Wallace, Mrs. John W. Ledbetter, Jr. holding J. Kelly, Johnette standing and James Eugene on the right.

THE CHESTER JACK MADSEN FAMILY

Both Jack and Joyce Madsen are lifetime members of the Round Rock community. They operate a dairy northeast of Round Rock with 80 dairy cows. Above is a family photo with Russell, Leslie, Mrs. Joyce Madsen and Mr. Jack Madsen in front. In back are Robert, Ronald and Larry. The picture at the bottom has Joyce and Russell in front, Jack, Mrs. Leslie (Cheryl) Madsen, Robert, Leslie, and Ronald with pet cow, "Betsy."

SAMUEL E. MERCER, JR. FAMILY. Stephanie, Ruby, Ava, Mr. Samuel and Mrs. Clara Mercer, Samantha, Dennis and Cassandra. The Mercer live at 302 West Logan Street.

ON LEFT
Garthaniel Mercer

ON RIGHT
Nathaniel Mercer, Violet Mercer Caldwell, Samuel Mercer, Sr. standing. Beatrice Mercer Mays, Matthew Mercer and Edan Mercer Johnson. These are children of Mr. and Mrs. Monroe Mercer. Picture made in 1938.

BELOW
SAMUEL E. MERCER, SR. FAMILY in 1942
Mrs. Willie Mercer, Carrie, Sam Jr., and Samuel Sr.

THE MARTIN E. PARKER FAMILY
Martin E., Frieda Lou, Terrence Lloyd, Laurie Lou, Martin G. "Skipper"
The Martin Parker's live in the Merrelltown community where he was born and reared. He and his wife Frieda, were married July 28, 1950. He is a career Post Office employee with over 28 years service and is Postmaster at the Round Rock Post Office.

MARTIN G. "SKIPPER" AND KATHY PARKER

JAMES RONALD AND LAURIE PARKER McELROY

Both are students at Stephen F. Austin University at Nacogdoches. Kathy is the former Kathy Schafer of Canadian, Texas.

Both are students at Stephen F. Austin University at Nacogdoches. James Ronald is from Pineland, Texas.

THE WILLIAM E. PARKER FAMILY

Picture was made in 1936. The Parker family is an old pioneer family that came to Texas from Tennessee in 1880. After settling in the Merrelltown community, there have been several generations grow up there including this family.

William "Willie" E. & Dorthy are seated with Edith, Loraine, Martin and Jack standing with Bertha Faye in front.

THE W. E. PARKER FAMILY
in 1972

After retiring from farming and ranching for 50 years in the Merrelltown community, Willie and Dorthy Parker sold their farm and retired to live at 211 West Main St. in Round Rock, Texas. Picture on right is the same family as above only 36 years later.

ABOVE
PEARSON, Ivean, Pauline (Ranchers)
RIGHT—TOP TO BOTTOM
BANKS, Jeffrey (Technician), Ivalene nee Pearson (RRHS '68)
ENGLAND, Joe F. (Research), Claretta, nee Pearson (RRHS '59), Joe M. and Dale.
DAVIS, Chuck (Insurance), Ruth, nee England (RRHS '60), Mark, Stacey
BELOW:
ENGLAND, Kenneth (Minister), Elsa (RRISD Faculty)

THE VIRGIL RABB FAMILY: Nancy, Casi, Cody, Cary and Virgil

THE VIRGIL RABB HOME, "CASA ROCA"
Located on Highway 79 at Palm Valley, just East of Round Rock.

LUTHER O. AND LA UNA RAMSEY

Mr. Luther O. Ramsey was born on April 17, 1890 in Maddenville, Pennsylvania. He joined the U.S. Army and came to Texas in 1912 to fight Pancho Villa, as the first Quartermaster Sergeant in the U.S. Army. Instead of finding the Mexican outlaw, he found a young lady by the name of LaUna Ferrell, a school teacher, and they were married March 15, 1915. They have 2 daughters, Lurlene Merrell of Leander and Nayrue Pridgeon of Houston. After leaving the Army, Mr. Ramsey came to Round Rock in 1916. He served many years on the Round Rock Volunteer Fire Department. He was Fire Marshal for years. Mr. Ramsey served on the Round Rock Independent School Board for several years as member and also as president. Upon retirement from the board, he was commissioned as tax collector and served many years with Mrs. Ramsey as his assistant. He worked for the I&GN Railroad Co. from 1916 until 1919 as a steam shovel engineer. In 1925, he went to work for the J. C. Jackson Furniture Store and Undertaking Parlor until 1943. During WW II, he worked in Alaska for a construction firm. Mr. Ramsey served on the city council for many years and has been active in community affairs for the past 52 years. Mr. Ramsey is the only known Round Rock citizen for whom an extra edition of the Round Rock Leader was published. The editor had told him that if he was elected as City Marshal, the special issue would be published.

THE GUS W. SAGER FAMILY

STANDING IN BACK: The family of Pastor Wilfred Sager, Sioux Falls, South Dakota.
SITTING ON LEFT: The family of Pastor Earl Eliason, Houston, Texas.
IN CENTER: Pastor and Mrs. Gus W. Sager, Round Rock, Texas.
SITTING AND STANDING ON RIGHT: The family of Dr. Allan Sager, Fort Worth, Texas.

GUS W. SAGER
Supt. and Chaplain, in the new Chapel of Trinity Lutheran Home.
Years 1959-1964.

The newly constructed Chapel in 1962.

THE RUDOLPH A. SELLSTROM FAMILY

Rudolph and Beda—UPPER LEFT.
UPPER RIGHT: Beda with her famous Swedish coffee cake. Won reserve grand champion award in Fourth Annual Bake Show at Travis County Pecan Growers Show.

ABOVE: George, Jimmy, Rudolph, Beda, Gloria Marie and Ginger.

LEFT: Beda with a few of her prize winning ribbons won for Swedish coffee cakes, bread, candy, cookies and fruit and vegetables.

The Sellstroms have lived on the same farm over 50 years on F.M. 1325. Both were born and reared at Round Rock. Rudolph was the son of Mr. and Mrs. Carl A. Sellstrom. Beda the daughter of Mr. and Mrs. John Stark.

The Marion F. Womble Family

MRS. WOMBLE
S. A., Tony, Lerlene

Tony, June, Everett, Sarah, Lynn Womble

Anthony Lynn Womble
1960 Round Rock Graduate

Richard, Lerlene, Claire, Ricky Ward

Richard Ward, Jr.
1966 Round Rock Graduate

Eva and S. A. Womble

Danny

Suzanne Womble
Edcouch-Elsa Soph.

Samuel Marion Womble
Edcouch-Elsa Graduate

Danuel Allen Womble
Edcouch-Elsa Graduate

David Evan Womble
Edcouch-Elsa Junior

Connie Rex, Peggy, Dusty, Renae Womble

Connie Rex Womble
1951 Round Rock Graduate

MR. AND MRS. HENRY CLEVE WARREN

Both Cleve and Cora Warren are members of pioneer families of the Round Rock vicinity. Mr. Warren is a son of the late Mr. and Mrs. J. R. Warren of the Rutledge community. Mrs. Warren was a daughter of the late Mr. and Mrs. Paul Hester. Both have lived in and around Round Rock all of their life. They observed their 50th wedding anniversary February 5, 1972. They have a family of six children. All are graduates of Round Rock High School as well as their mother who graudated in 1921. Pictured below: Henry Paul Warren, Mary Frances Warren McNeese, Willie Bernice Warren Thomas, Betty Jo Warren Peterson, Doris Jean Warren Reid, and Patsy Ruth Warren Williams, the children of Mr. and Mrs. H. C. Warren, 110 South Sheppard.

THE FRANKLIN M. ANDERSON FAMILY
Michael, Franklin, Joyce and Karen.   The Andersons live at 305 West Anderson.

THE JOE D. ANDERSON FAMILY
Dianne, Mr. Joe D. Anderson, Mrs. Vera Anderson and Darwin enjoy the den of their home.

THE ROBERT BAIRRINGTON FAMILY
Wanda and Robert with Mike and Ronnie in front. Came to Round Rock in 1966 from Waco.

THE OLIVER BERGLUND FAMILY
Rev. Berglund is pastor of the Palm Valley Lutheran Church. Daughters Cheryl, Bonnie, Susan and Valerie stand in back. In front, Paul, Pastor Oliver Berglund, Mrs. Genevieve Berglund and Mark.

WILLIAM McKENZIE BOWDEN
1869-1930

Mr. Bowden was born February 28, 1869, and orphaned at the age of three. He was reared in the home of Dr. Black of Round Rock. His first job was working on the construction of the state capitol in Austin.

He married Miss Ida Robinson of Austin and four children, Jennie, Margaret, William and Charles were born into the family.

Mr. Bowden was employed by the Bell Telephone Company and he served as manager of the Round Rock Telephone Office from 1907 until his retirement about 20 years later.

THE EDDIE BREAUX FAMILY
L.–R.: Cne, Mrs. Jan Breaux, Angela, Von, Mr. Eddie Breaux and Deedee.–501 Karolyn

THE HAROLD D. BREDTHAUER FAMILY
Kurt and wife Zosia Bredthauer on left, Jill, June Walsh Bredthauer and Mr. Harold D.

THE GEORGE A. BUJNOCH FAMILY
George Bujnoch is Principal of the middle school and his wife Genevieve is a native of Germany. The Bujnochs came to Round Rock in 1970. Their children, Maurice and Jennifer, and the Bujnoch family live at 1007 Tanglewood. Hometowns, Shiner, Texas.

MR. EDDIE B. AND HEDDA
BURKLUND

Picture
made
February 20, 1924.

Their twin daughters Genevive and Jan-
ette are graduates of Round Rock High
School.

THE LUZ CASTILLO, SR. FAMILY

Luz Castillo, Sr. on the left and Mrs. Francisca Castillo on the right holding son John and baby daughter Olivia stands by her side. Pictures
made in the early 1940's.

THE AARON CLUCK FAMILY
David, Aaron, Betty and Surita Cluck. The Clucks live in the Summitt Oaks Community.

THE ELMER A. COTTRELLS
Elmer and Viola Cottrell live at 404 N. Georgetown. They moved to Round Rock in 1948. They have two children, Major David Dean Cottrell and Mrs. Jerry (Arlene) Miles.

THE M. J. COWAN FAMILY
Ricky, LaRue, Jan, Mr. M. J. Cowan and Donna
The M. J. Cowan family live at 101 Vista Ave.

ROBERT AND STELLA EGGER

Both Mr. and Mrs. Egger are members of
pioneer families. They are owners and
developers of Egger Acres. This acreage has
been in the Egger family since 1896.

They have one daughter, Mrs. Lawrence
(Willie Mae) Pfluger.

THE MILTON T. "TUBBY" FERRELL FAMILY

Milton "Tubby" Ferrell holds granddaughter Sherry Summers, Delphine Schoen Ferrell daughter Pat Summers and son, Sonny Ferrell.

DR. AND MRS. DICK B. GREGG

Dr. Gregg, long time family doctor of the Round Rock community and surrounding area, holds daughter Susan at Christmas of 1941.

THE NOEL GRISHAM FAMILY

ON LEFT: Joan, Jane and Jean, daughters of Mr. and Mrs. Noel Grisham, stand in front of their home at 404 E. Main Street with Mrs. Helen Grisham and Mr. Noel Grisham, Superintendent of Round Rock Schools.

THE LEONARD HEDRICK FAMILY
Lacey on left, Mrs. Lytane Hedrick, Lesa, Mr. Leonard Hedrick and Laurie. The Hedricks live at 505 Karolyn. They came to Round Rock in 1971 from Midland.

THE DALE HESTER FAMILY

Pamela and Brian stand in front of their parents, Bess and Dale Hester. Mr. Hester has been Mayor of Round Rock since 1969. They live at 803 Timberwood.

THE DONALD HESTER FAMILY

Mr. Don Hester, Jeff, Steven, Robin and Betty Sellstrom Hester with Shelley in front. The Hesters own the Dairy Kreme and they live at 908 Summit Drive.

ROBERT E. AND IRENE JOHNSON

Mr. Johnson worked as a farmer and also worked at the Round Rock Post Office over 28 years. Mr. Johnson was Postmaster for nearly 25 years.

Mrs. Johnson was the former Irene Neese and taught second grade at Round Rock from 1930 until 1934.

They have one son, Robert E. Johnson, Jr.

THE J. H. KAVANAUGH FAMILY

SEATED: Mrs. J. H. Kavanaugh, Mr. J. H. Kavanaugh and May.

SECOND ROW: W. O. Schultz, Mrs. W. O. Schultz, Mrs. Bill Kavanaugh, Mrs. James Wilson.

BACK ROW: Mrs. John Henry Kavanaugh, John Henry Kavanaugh, Bill L. Kavanaugh, James Wilson.

This picture was taken in the spring of 1955

The J. H. Kavanaugh family has been the owners and publishers of the weekly hometown newspaper, Round Rock Leader, since October of 1929—over 42 years of continuous service to the Round Rock community and surrounding area. May Kavanaugh still puts out the Round Rock Leader each Thursday with the help of the family.

THE WAYNE T. KING FAMILY

Mrs. Doris King holding Dana, Mr. Wayne King and Sherri with Glenda in front. The Wayne T. Kings live at 1000 Tanglewood.

THE WILLIAM R. KITTS FAMILY

William R. Kitts, Mrs. Kay Kitts, Teresa, Monica on back row with Gaila, Wade and Tamie in front. The Bill Kitts live at 507 Karolyn.

RUSSELL AND CLARA KOONTZ

The Koontz's live just West of Round Rock on F.M. 620 by the new High School

THE JIMMY JOE KRAMER FAMILY

Mr. Joe Kramer, Mrs. Pat Sellstrom Kramer and daughters Kimberly Kay and Karen. The Kramers live just north of Round Rock in their country home.

DURWOOD AND DELIA LANE
The Lanes are long time residents of Round Rock and presently live at 402 Round Rock Ave.

THE CARTER LESTER AND THE BRUCE KIRTLEY FAMILIES
On left, Bruce Kirtley holds son Scott and Mrs. Judy Kirtley. Mr. Carter Lester, daughter Jane and Mrs. Trudy Lester. Judy Kirtley is daughter of Carter and Trudy. The Lesters own and operate Doublecreek Farms on Gattis School Road.

THE ISAAC LOPEZ FAMILY

Mr. Issac Lopez and Mrs. Ellen Pena Lopez with son Matthew. Mr. Lopez is presently serving as trustee for the Round Rock Independent School District.

THE WALLACE LUERSON FAMILY

Mrs. Jo Ann Luerson, Kevin and Mr. Wallace Luerson in their home by Dove Creek, southeast of Round Rock. Mr. Luerson built their own home.

THE WINFRED G. "WHIMPY" McCOY FAMILY

Mrs. Joyce McCoy and Whimpy McCoy with their children, Shelley, Timothy and Jeff. Mr. McCoy is manager of the Texas Power and Light Co. Their home is at 514 Karolyn.

THE C. THOMAS NEWSOM FAMILY

Mr. C. Thomas Newsom is Director, Department of Religious Life, at the Texas Baptist Children Home. Their son Brad and daughter Amy and Mrs. Jane Newsom. 506 West Oak Dr.

L. P. "BUD" AND CORA PARKER

Mr. and Mrs. L. P. "Bud" Parker live at 302 Sunset Drive. They have three sons, Joe, Marvin and Gene. Both are lifelong residents of the Round Rock area. They celebrated 50th wedding anniversary December 18, 1971.

THE CHRIS PEREZ FAMILY

Rose Marie, Mr. Chris Perez, Jessie, Joe Anthony, Mrs. Linda Perez and Chris, Jr. Chris and Linda own and operate Chris & Linda's Beauty Shoppe and Hair Style Center.

227

THE ROBERT L. PETERS, JR. FAMILY

Dr. Robert L. Peters, Jr. is the community doctor and their residence is at 909 Summit. Children Rex, Janice and Becky with Mrs. Ruby Peters and Dr. R. L. Peters.

THE C. ARNOLD PETERSON FAMILY

Mr. Peterson is the photographer we can all thank for making the pictures that are seen in this book. Professionally, he is Principal of Pond Springs Elementary School. Mrs. Wilma Peterson is Principal of Southside Elementary. Son Allan is student at Round Rock High School.

DR. AND MRS. JAMES H. PORTER stand in front of one of the older stone houses in Round Rock, located west of the St. Charles Hotel. They are currently restoring this home. In 1873, it was the birthplace of Dudley S. Barker, Texas Ranger & Sheriff.

CLARENCE J. AND ESTELLE ROBERTS
Clarence Roberts, a truck broker, traveled all over the United States. He hauled all instruments to N.A.S.A. in Houston for all the moon trips. He also hauled radar into Canada. Mr. Roberts was bonded and cleared by the F.B.I. Mr. and Mrs. Roberts live in their home at 610 East Oak Drive.

THE JOHN D. ROBERTSON, SR., THE JOHN D. ROBERTSON, JR. AND THE JAMES G. PETERS FAMILY

BACK ROW: Jim and Jolene Peters; Barry, David, Sarah and John D. Robertson, Jr. holding Randy. FRONT: Jayme and James Peters, Mrs. John D. Robertson, Johnnie, John D. Robertson, Sr. and Mark. Picture of flood of 1913 is work of artist Mrs. Bennie Stark, sister of John D. Robertson, Sr.

THE VICTOR A. ROBERTSON, JR. FAMILY

Larry, Gary, Sharon and Karen with Mrs. Ann Robertson and Mr. Victor Robertson, Jr. The Robertsons live at 506 W. Austin. Mr. Robertson is owner of the Vic Robertson Grocery. He is also president of the Round Rock High School Board.

JOHNNIE C. AND CLARA ROEPKE

The Roepkes came to Round Rock in 1958. Their hometown is Thorndale. Mr. Roepke is Constable for the Round Rock area. The Roepkes live on Fairlane Drive.

THE V. RAY SANDERS FAMILY

The Sanders live at McNeil where he is postmaster and manages the McNeil Store. Their children are Arthur, Shirley and Marc, being held by Mr. Sanders. Mrs. Dorothy Sanders on the right. Mr. Sanders is a member of the Round Rock School Board.

THE J. W. SAVAGE FAMILY

The J. W. Savage family live in the Jollyville community but are very much a part of Round Rock and its activities. J. W. Savage, Garland, who is a student at Round Rock High School and Mrs. Nig Savage.

THE RAYMOND SELLSTROM FAMILY

On left is Marc Cummings and Linda with their son Ray. Mr. Raymond Sellstrom and Mrs. Edith Sellstrom on the right. Linda is the daughter of the Sellstroms. Both Mr. and Mrs. Sellstrom are lifetime residents of Round Rock. Mr. Sellstrom is a local paint contractor.

THE CHARLES W. STARK FAMILY

FRONT: Charlene, Jo Anna, Wanda, Stacy. BACK: Neal Lynch holding Thomas and Linda Lynch; Tommie, Mrs. Jo Ann Stark holding Shelly and Mr. Charles W. Stark.

FLORENCE STULKEN

Florence Stulken started teaching at the University of Texas School of Business in 1919 and taught until 1958. She owns and operates her farm and ranch on F.M. Road 620 west of Round Rock. She purchased this farm and ranch in 1953 and retired to live with her "pets."

THE JAMES D. TOUNGATE FAMILY

Mrs. Melvalyn Toungate, Darrell, Dana, Melissa and Mr. James D. Toungate in their home at 1009 Tanglewood. Mr. Toungate is a member of the Round Rock City Council.

THE VONNIE J. TUCKER FAMILY

Mr. Vonnie Tucker and Mrs. Jonelle Tucker live north of Egger Acres in their farm home. Tim and Jean Ann are students at Round Rock, where Mr. Tucker is a teacher.

THE JERRY WALL FAMILY

The Jerry Wall family in their home at 520 Karolyn. David, Mr. Jerry Wall, Perry, Mrs. Glenda Wall and Ronnie. The Walls are builders and real estate dealers.

THE JAMES D. WATSON FAMILY

The Watson family came to Round Rock in 1965 as pastor for the First Baptist Church. They served until January of 1972. The Watsons are now preparing for foreign mission work. Glen Ray, Mrs. Margie Watson, Grady, Pastor James Watson and Delane.

THE NORMAN G. WHITLOW FAMILY

The Norman G. "Bunky" Whitlow's have been Round Rock residents since 1949. Mrs. Geneva Whitlow, Stuart, Scott, Mr. "Bunky" Whitlow and Sandy in their home at 507 West Oak. Mr. N. G. Whitlow is President of Farmers State Bank.

THE RAY WOYTEK FAMILY

Ronald, Mr. Ray Woytek, Mrs. Ella Mae Woytek, Teri with Robert and Carla in front. Mrs. Woytek is the former Ella Mae Anderson. The Woyteks have local Insurance Agency.

CODY AND RUBY ADOLPHSON
709 Round Rock Ave.

NOLAN E. AND WINONA BALCH
Danny and Debra—400 Sunset

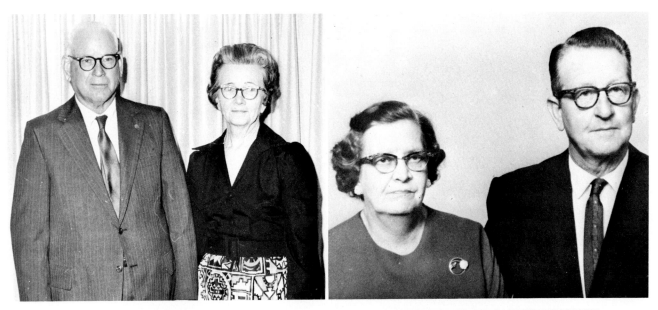

CARL G. AND INEZ BEARD
604 East Main

REYNOLD "RAY" AND PAULINE BERGLUND
109 North Lewis

ANTON H. BERKMAN
Born in Round Rock 1897—Retired professor

WILL A. AND FANNIE BLAIR
Merchant in 1900 at 101 East Main Street.

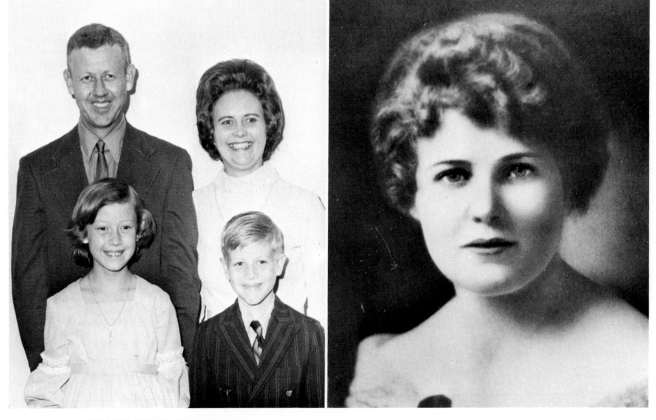

WELDON AND MARY BURKLUND
Sharon and Gary   609 East Oak Drive

AGNES CARLSON
Picture made in 1917—109 S. Sheppard.

MRS. MARTHA CARLSON
101 Bellaire Circle

JOHN D. AND SHERRY COLLINS
1005 Tanglewood

FLOYD AND LINDA HACKER
Karen and Tina   1400 Robb Lane

HENRY AND GERALDINE HEISCH
Jeanie, Rodney, Rory, Randy   309 Vista

MR. AND MRS. BOB HORTON, SR.
Picture made in 1920 in Round Rock

ROY A. AND NINA F. KRIENKE
1001 Glenwood

MRS. THEO (ANITA) KRIENKE
515 West Oak

A. JOE JOHNSON
Born in Round Rock in 1882—110 W. Logan

DWIGHT AND NANCY LAMB

with daughter Heather   508 East Main

MRS. CARRIE MADSEN
710 East Liberty

MR. AND MRS. HARRY MADSEN

Gary and Jimmy   806 East Main

VIRGIL AND BARBARA McCASLAND
David and Doug   1111 Northwest

RON AND GLENDA MORRISON
Both are lifelong residents of Round Rock

MR. AND MRS. GRANT T. MILLEGAN
Married in Jollyville, 1930—210 College

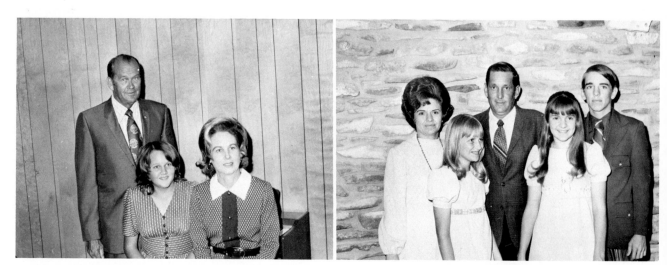

C. L. "TEX" AND BETSY NEHRING

Daughter Lisa   304 Brairwood St.

PAUL AND MOZELLE NICKS
Brenda, Diane, Glendon—510 West Oak Dr.

FRED AND BEATRICE OLSON
Two sons: Marvin & Mike—507 W. Liberty

HARRY AND SELMA NOREN
Married December 30, 1925. One son, Morris

MIKE H. AND MARY OLSON
Mike Jr., Stephen and Cindy

GENE A. AND DELORES PARKER
Daughter Deborah   523 Karolyn

JOHN AND MILDRED POWELL
1401 Circle Drive

ROBERT L. AND BILLIE JO REED
Sons Robert Jr., John   705 East Austin

MR. AND MRS. JOSEPH REPA, SR.
608 Karolyn

ROBERT W. AND MARY RICHMOND
Tom and Steve in back—Becky and Gary front.

DuWAYNE AND CAROL SANDEL
516 Karolyn

DON AND DONNA SANDERS
Sons Ron, Jim and Jeff

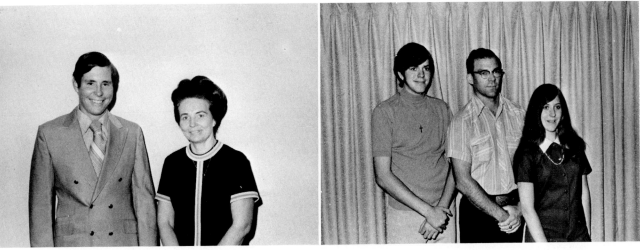

MRS. VERA SCOTT AND SON CARLTON
Came to Round Rock in 1964 from Dallas

MR. EARL SEAY, MIKE AND DEBBYE SUE
1003 Glenwood

TED AND GWEN SELBY
Daughter Shana and son Mark

DENNIS AND ANN TEMPLETON
Both are teachers in the Round Rock Schools

MRS. W. J. WALSH
Daughters: June Bredthauer & Regina Knox

MRS. ELLEN WARNER
She lives in Palm Valley

PHILIP AND ALIENN WARNER
Son, Paul.   Their daughter, Nancy Lamb

ARTHUR AND VIRGINIA WOODS
David and Carolyn

THE THEODORE J. ZIMMERMAN, JR. FAMILY
Mr. Theo Zimmerman, Jr., Mrs. Betty Zimmerman holding Lee and Jason in front.

HUMAN INTEREST

THE BRUSHY CREEK CHARCOAL BURNERS

MRS. JEAN BUSTIN
AND
MRS. DELPHINE FERRELL
in their Cadillac
"float"
FRONTIER DAYS 1969

BELOW
Jean & Delphine "clown it up"
on Main Street during
FRONTIER DAYS

THIS PAGE COMPLIMENTS OF BIG G'S NIGHT CLUB.

PARADE MARSHAL
N. G. "Bunky" Whitlow, Mrs. Geneva Whitlow and Sandy Whitlow

A Real Frontier Family.

Mr. Everett Clark in the wagon, driver of the team.

Scott & Stewart Whitlow having fun in the little "tin lizzy."

THE TWO TOP PICTURES COMPLIMENTS OF THE N. G. WHITLOW FAMILY

MELODRAMA ON THE STREET
"The Fight to Save the Farm"

STARRING
Nancy Rabb as the mother, Billye Jo Reed as the Heroine, Geneva Whitlow as the Hero.

FRONTIER DAY
1968

LOWER PICTURE COMPLIMENTS OF MRS. BILLYE JO REED

CRAZY HORSE SALOON 1971

Picture on left above: Pam Hester, daughter of Mr. and Mrs. Dale Hester, and Jan Beck daughter of Mr. and Mrs. E. O. Beck in front with Kelley, Diane & Debbie Sessler, the daughters of Mr. and Mrs. Marvin Sessler and Rose Mary Perez, the daughter of Mr. and Mrs. Chris Perez. Kay Beck swings in the swing in the picture at upper right.

FRONTIER DAYS 1971 COSTUME WINNERS. Front: Brenda, Richard & Edward Steen, Carla Noren, Brian Hester-on horse-, Clem Runnels. BACK ROW: Mrs. W. H. Ransom & children, Mr. and Mrs. David Houston, Bertha Johnson, Jerry Harlow, Katrina Davis, Mary Fellows and Darlene Waters.

THIS PAGE COMPLIMENTS OF BILL HALO HEATING & AIR CONDITIONING

FIRST GRADE IN 1929. Xenia Voigt teacher and P.E. Dickson, Superintendent. FRONT: Unknown, Unknown, Warren Kaufman, Unknown, Alton Prewitt, Edward Stark, Glen Warren, Johnnie Schmitt, Milton Krienke. MIDDLE: Unknown, Unknown, Artie Louise Ferrell, Gladys Youngbloom, Lillianette McNeese, Velda Ruth Hill, Emma Jean Hamilton, Kathrine Brown, Maudie Fields, Dorthy Mae Whitely, Gladys Anderson, Mary Sansom. BACK ROW: Tony Schmidt, Isaac Perez, Louise Stobaugh, Luther Ross, Unknown, Unknown, Enos Martinez, George Woolsey, Unknown, Frank McNeese, Billy Sellstrom and Bessie Hester.
PICTURE COMPLIMENTS OF DORTHY MAE WHITELEY MARTIN

ROUND ROCK TWIRLING CLUB. Won 2nd place in U.S.T.A. Texas State Twirling Contest in small team division in June of 1970. Held at Austin, Texas. L to R: Candy Gibson, Laurie Parker, Joan Zimmerman, Debbie Stark, Brenda Traugott and Patty Armstrong.

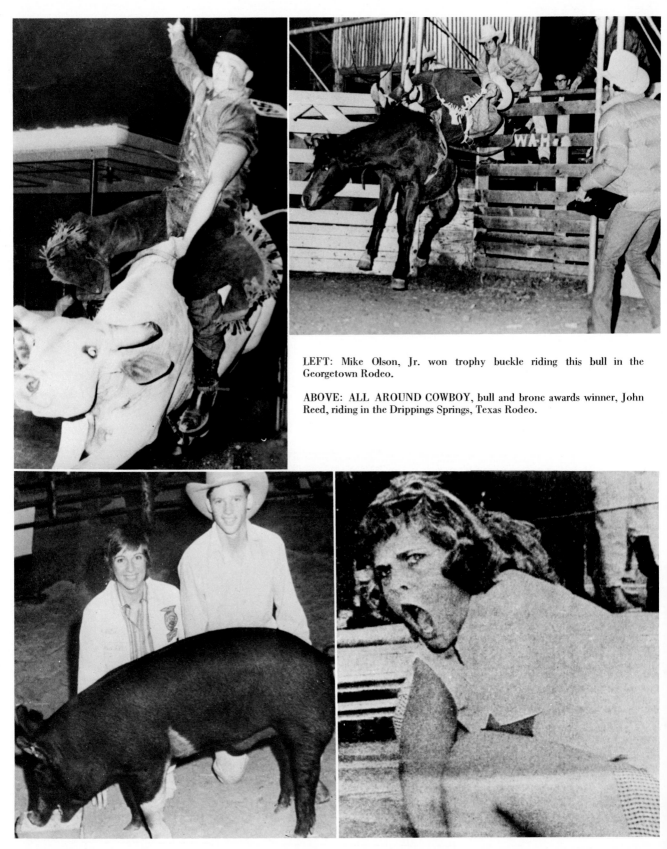

LEFT: Mike Olson, Jr. won trophy buckle riding this bull in the Georgetown Rodeo.

ABOVE: ALL AROUND COWBOY, bull and bronc awards winner, John Reed, riding in the Drippings Springs, Texas Rodeo.

Terrence Lloyd Parker with his prize winning pig "Wilbur" at the Taylor 1972 Livestock Show. FFA Sweetheart Jane Lester.

Patsy Bassford on June 15, 1961 as she races with the Round Rock Womens Fire Dept. pumper team. "Turn that water off."

Kay the Twirler

Regan the Ballplayer

Jan the Tapper

Jan, Regan and Kay Beck ready for the Pinewood Derby

Gunslingers I. G. Janca III & Regan Beck.

Gene Beck and his ranch hands

John Reed, 1965—Any Indian can kill a deer—just chiefs get turkeys.

253

ABOVE: John Ledbetter, V "Going Fishing"

UPPER RIGHT: Gena Kathryn Antill JUNIOR MISS CHRISTMAS 1970

Gena Kathryn Antill, Bernice Anne Antill and Johnette Ledbetter proudly stand by after unveiling the State Historical Marker for the Round Rock. 11-7-71.

Craig and Coleen Toungate, son and daughter of Mr. & Mrs. Lum Toungate and Terry Parker, son of Mr. and Mrs. Martin E. Parker, perform in the Crazy Horse Saloon during Frontier Days, 1971.

COMPLIMENTS OF MR. AND MRS. LUM TOUNGATE

CRAZY HORSE CHORUS LINE

Janet Henna, Linda Coward, Linda Daniel, Nancy Nelson, Carol Ruth Henna, Kathy Olson, Debbie Callison, Diane Coward, and Gail Malmstrom in front.

FRONTIER DAYS 1968

COMPLIMENTS MRS. LOUIS HENNA

CHARCOAL BURNERS PERFORM IN CRAZY HORSE SALOON 1966

Jean Bustin, Delphine Ferrell, Ruth Burleson & Laura Davol.

COMPLIMENTS LAURA DAVOL

1969 BEAUTY PAGEANT
L to R: Sherry Hagee, Runner-Up, Kathy Olson, Miss Round Rock 1969, Lupe Medrano and Kathy Savage.

COMPLIMENTS OF WOMANS CLUB

MISS LINDA DANIEL
MISS ROUND ROCK OF 1970
Popular RRHS student. Was cheerleader, Homecoming queen, class favorite, Member Honor Society, Outstanding Senior

COMPLIMENTS MR. AND MRS. BEN BUSTIN

MISS CINDY OLSON
Daughter of Mr. and Mrs. Mike Olson, as she appeared in the 1970 Beauty Pageant. Cindy won Miss Talent and was 1st Runner-Up for Miss Petite.

COMPLIMENTS OF MRS. IMA LENTZ

FOUR GENERATIONS ATTENDED MERRELLTOWN SCHOOL

The Merrelltown school has been in operation for over 100 years. Pictured at left is four generations that went to school there. Mrs. Lura King, seated, started there in 1872; her daughter on right, Mrs. Stella Hester; her daughter Mrs. Willie Parker is on the left; and her daughter Mrs. Edith Parker Finney in the center. This picture was made in 1955. The Merrelltown school consolidated with the Round Rock School District in 1945. Since that date, the building is used as a community center.

COMPLIMENTS MRS. W. E. PARKER

1967 FRONTIER DAYS OFFICIALS AND JUDGES. L to R: R. L. Chilton, Olivia Castillo, Mrs. Margaret Carlson, Nell Marie Burkland, Mayor Elmer Cottrell, Miss Round Rock of 1967, Nancy Jo Warner, Congressman J. J. "Jake" Pickle, Jane Nelson & Glyn Morsbach.

THE CARP KINGS

Mr. D. B. Lane and "Uncle" Luke Robertson have their fishing gear and prepare to
land a few fish. They made their own
Do-Bait, used in fishing for carps, to fish
with and to sell.

COMPLIMENTS OF MRS. D. B. LANE

ABOVE: Murry Deison, on right, with Frank
Warren, Mrs. O. H. McAdams son-in-law, on deer
hunt at Fort Stockton Ranch Lodge.

LOWER RIGHT: Rev. R. A. Deison, Davis
Deison, Leon Carlson and Murry Deison display a
catch of fish taken at Buchanan Dam.

COMPLIMENTS OF MRS. THELMA DEISON

MR. WILLIE PARKER—1970
With largest deer he ever killed. Dressed 160 pounds. Killed in south Texas.

NANCY JO WARNER
CRAZY HORSE SALOON dancer and later voted MISS ROUND ROCK 1967

Postmaster Martin E. Parker with his 1968 ZIP CODE FLOAT.

Virgil Rabb gets a hit and goes to first base—WUPS!!—Virgil gets thrown!!

Vonnie Tucker scores a run.

Buddy Fredrickson didn't make it!

President Martin E. Parker makes it O.K.

Sonny Balch had his ups and downs

Sam Bass (Bobby King), his partners Barnes (Otis Lawrence) & Jackson (Dobie Herring) ride in to rob the bank.

Texas Ranger Captain Jones, (M. T. "Tubby" Ferrell) looks over the situation before challenging the band of robbers.

Sam Bass doesn't like questioning and gunfire takes place and the town deputies, Buddy Fredrickson and Dennis Teague fall.

The wounded Sam Bass and his partners ride out of town as fast as their horses would take them. Informer was Kurt Bredthauer.

Sam Bass struggles to stay on his horse and escape at the same time.

Rangers (W. Carroll Allen, Jr.) in front and (Bill Tisdale) with guns firing at bandits.

Round Rock is Our

RALPH SWEET

The Sweet Publishing Company, Inc. is an independent religious publishing company. We produce sunday school materials, a newspaper, a magazine, books and other supplies for churches. We market in every state and in many foreign countries.

The printing for our company has been done by various printing com-

 SWEET PUBLISHING

Kind of Town

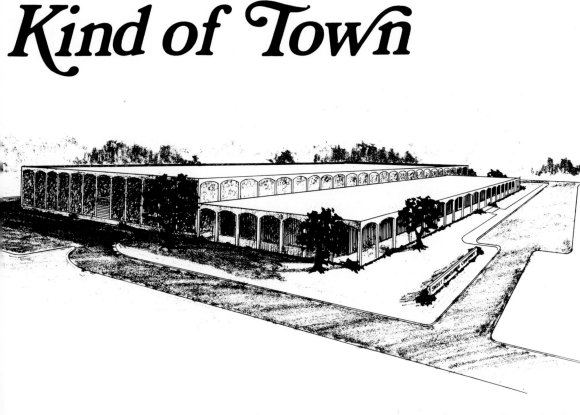

panies in several states. We will combine this in our Round Rock plant. We will also do printing for other publishers and for general commercial clients.

Our metal stamping division will manufacture communion ware. Our plastic manufacturing division will have an initial capacity of 250,000 parts per day.

We look forward to being a part of Round Rock. We certainly appreciate the hospitality and encouragement shown to us by the wonderful people of this community.

Ralph Sweet, President

COMPANY

The next 32 pages of ROUND ROCK, TEXAS, U.S.A.!!!, is being made available through the courtesy of R. B. Sweet Publishing Co. As this book goes to press, the Sweet Publishing Co. is in the process of building their plant in Round Rock. The Kiwanis Club of Round Rock wishes to thank Mr. R. B. Sweet for his help and guidance in the publication of this book.

These 32 pages were made in 1938 when off set printing was in its early stages and is being reproduced exactly as they were originally published. If the quality is not up to standard of the rest of this book, please understand the reason.

+ +

The Kiwanis Club of Round Rock, Texas would also like to acknowledge and show their appreciation to Rev. Vernon Perry, the Pastor of the Round Rock Methodist Church in 1938, for his foresight and efforts in preserving for us, the future generations of Round Rock, the history in picture and print of Round Rock from 1913 to 1938. Rev. Perry did all of the photography, art work, composing and the actual publication of these 32 pages. Rev. Perry is still a Methodist Pastor in the Southwest Texas Conference in 1972.

ROUND ROCK WHITE LIME CO.

CELEBRATING
25 YEARS OF
PROGRESS.....
Round Rock, Texas
1913–1938

This book is dedicated to those still living and to those now gone who have made possible by their foresight and labor the progress of these 25 years.

Photos by Vernon Perry

Round rock under the Old Town bridge for which Round Rock, Texas was named.

Louis Henna   Billy Henna   Harve Killen

2

City Hall and Fire Station

It is just 20 miles from this building to the Marshall Ford Dam - practically the same distance it is from Austin, Texas, to the dam.

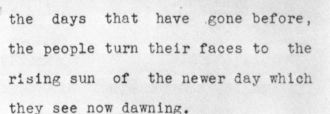

Marshall Ford Dam

Silver Anniversary

FROM A DIRTY little town with muddy streets, windmills, and kerosene lamps, the Round Rock of twenty-five years ago has grown into the thriving community its citizens of 1938 know and enjoy. Round Rock is proud of its past, proud of the progress which has marked the passing of the years, but, while recording briefly here those things which have been accomplished in the days that have gone before, the people turn their faces to the rising sun of the newer day which they see now dawning.

Beginning 25 years ago, with the incorporation of the town in 1913, a series of progressive steps marks the passing of the intervening years. A new three story brick school building in 1914 was the first development, followed in swift

(Turn to page 11)

3.

267

City of Round Rock

Former Mayors

1913

Jack Jordon
City Sec'y since
1914

1914

W. S. Brown

1924-25

C. V. Lansberry

1925-35

W. R. Woolsey

1938

R. B. Crimm

Mayor

M. L. Blacklock

City Council – 1938

H. N. Egger
Mayor Pro-tem.

T. E. Nelson

James Carlson

C. D. Anderson

W. T. Sowell

4.

Palm Valley
Lutheran Church

Pastor O. M. Bloom

Wilson Motor Company
Ford Dealers

W. C. Rightmer   H. P. Anderson

F. R. Wilson   M. G. Rightmer   Miss Lorraine Voigt   Eric Johnson   I. E. Simpson

269

W.T. Sowell
Service Station

SHELL

W.T. Sowell, Prop.   Alvin Fleischer   L.P. Parker

Baptist Church

Dr. Geo. Green

6

Methodist Church —

Rev. Vernon Perry

H. L. Stockbridge Grocery and Market

H. L. Stockbridge

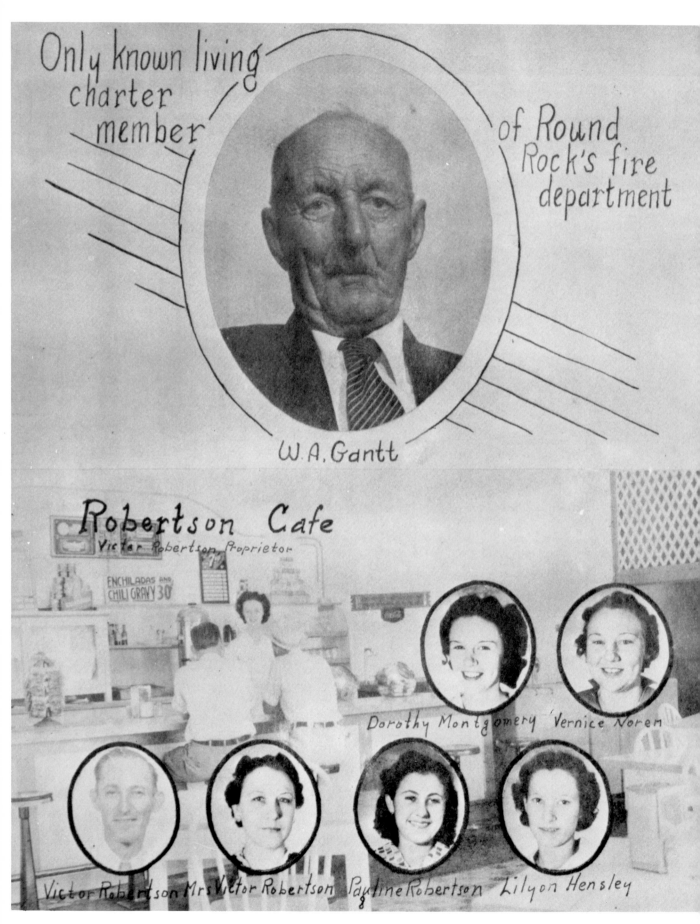

Only known living charter member of Round Rock's fire department

W. A. Gantt

Robertson Cafe
Victor Robertson, Proprietor

ENCHILADAS AND
CHILI GRAVY 30

Dorothy Montgomery   Vernice Norem

Victor Robertson   Mrs Victor Robertson   Pauline Robertson   Lilyon Hensley

Old and New in fire engines

Round Rock's first pumper is shown here. This old machine is now retired but may be seen on City Hall lawn. A Model "T" replaced it several years ago.

The Model "T" was, in its turn, replaced by the new engine shown below. This improvement came in 1938.

9.

Round Rock Fire Department

Chief 1913

O.A. Voigt

Fire Marshall

L.O. Ramsey

Chief 1938

C.D. Anderson

Former Chiefs

S.E. Loving

H.L. Stockbridge

Most of 1938 department shown here

10.

Round Rock School
of 25 years ago.

succession by paved highway through the town, electric lights about 15 years ago, a city-owned cotton yard, graveled and improved streets, Old Settlers Association moving headquarters here in 1923, another paved highway through town, natural gas, a city water system in 1936, a new City Hall and Fire Station immediately thereafter, a new $2500 fire engine in 1938, and just voted as this Anniversary Edition goes to press, a $90,000 city sewer project

(Turn to page 20)

Helmer Johnson

Jim Carlson

11

Present School Building

C. O. Britt
Superintendent

O. F. Terry
Principal

Noble Pharmacy

Planters Gin
has two plants in Round Rock
Insert is of larger plant
and its crew.

13

T.E. Nelson Home

S. & S. Grill

Johnnie Dailey   Bennie Price

Sam Sowell   Mrs Sam Sowell   Blanche Hill   "Tina" Burk   Lessie Lou Hicks

Round Rock School Board

Rev. Theo Kreinke G. R. Lundelius D. B. Gregg Helmer Johnson G. E. Peterson
President

P.T.A. President

A. H. Kaufman W. J. Walsh Dick Mayfield Mrs. J. W. Ledbetter

15

279

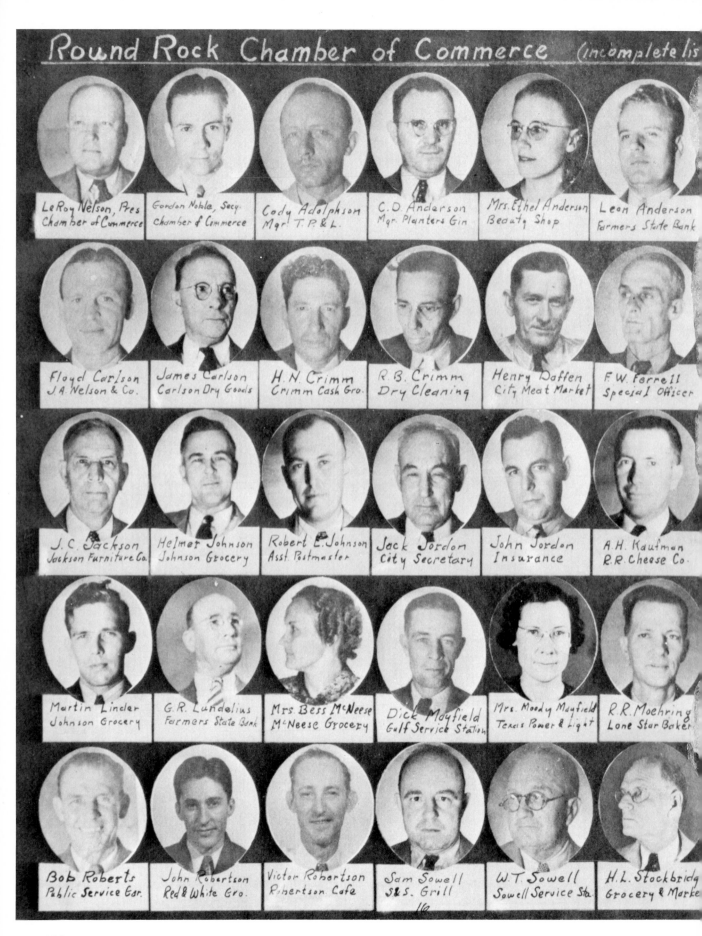

Round Rock Chamber of Commerce (incomplete lis

LeRoy Nelson, Pres.
Chamber of Commerce

Gordon Noble, Secy.
Chamber of Commerce

Cody Adolphson
Mgr. T.P.&L.

C.D. Anderson
Mgr. Planters Gin

Mrs. Ethel Anderson
Beauty Shop

Leon Anderson
Farmers State Bank

Floyd Carlson
J.A. Nelson & Co.

James Carlson
Carlson Dry Goods

H.N. Crimm
Crimm Cash Gro.

R.B. Crimm
Dry Cleaning

Henry Daffen
City Meat Market

F.W. Ferrell
Special Officer

J.C. Jackson
Jackson Furniture Co.

Helmer Johnson
Johnson Grocery

Robert E. Johnson
Asst. Postmaster

Jack Jordon
City Secretary

John Jordon
Insurance

A.H. Kaufman
R.R. Cheese Co.

Martin Linder
Johnson Grocery

G.R. Lundelius
Farmers State Bank

Mrs. Bess McNeese
McNeese Grocery

Dick Mayfield
Gulf Service Station

Mrs. Moody Mayfield
Texas Power & Light

R.R. Moehring
Lone Star Baker

Bob Roberts
Public Service Cor.

John Robertson
Red & White Gro.

Victor Robertson
Robertson Cafe

Sam Sowell
S&S. Grill

W.T. Sowell
Sowell Service Sta.

H.L. Stockbridge
Grocery & Marke

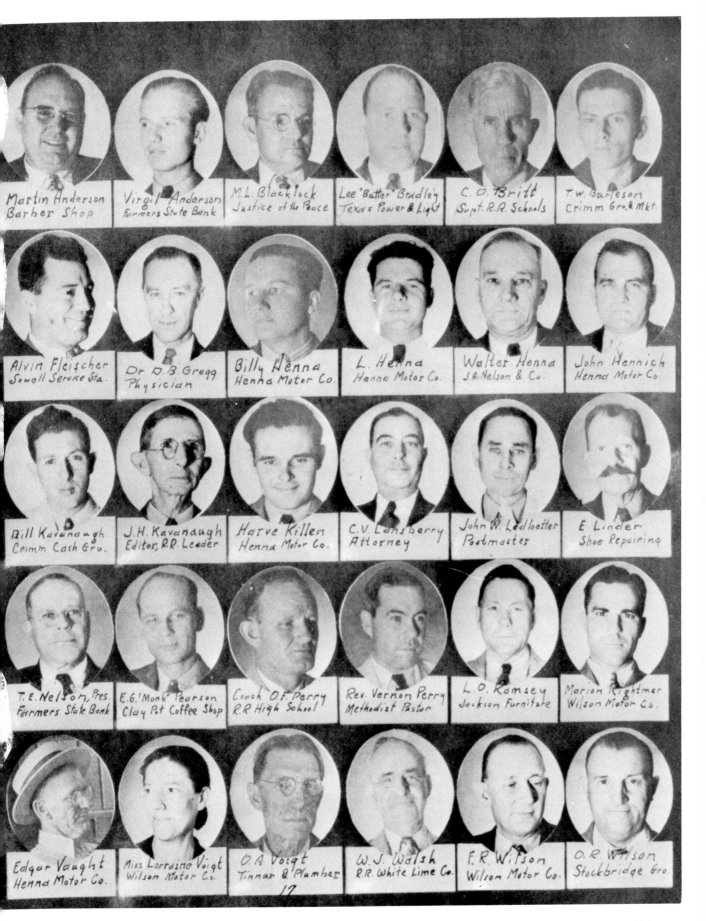

Martin Anderson
Barber Shop

Virgil Anderson
Farmers State Bank

M. L. Blacklock
Justice of the Peace

Lee "Butter" Bradley
Texas Power & Light

C. O. Britt
Supt. R.R. Schools

T. W. Burleson
Crimm Gro. & Mkt.

Alvin Fleischer
Sowell Service Sta.

Dr. D. B. Gregg
Physician

Billy Henna
Henna Motor Co.

L. Henna
Henna Motor Co.

Walter Henna
J. A. Nelson & Co.

John Hennich
Henna Motor Co.

Bill Kavanaugh
Crimm Cash Gro.

J. H. Kavanaugh
Editor, R.R. Leader

Harve Killen
Henna Motor Co.

C. V. Lansberry
Attorney

John W. Ledbetter
Postmaster

E. Linder
Shoe Repairing

T. E. Nelson, Pres.
Farmers State Bank

E. G. "Monk" Pearson
Clay Pot Coffee Shop

Coach O. F. Perry
R.R. High School

Rev. Vernon Perry
Methodist Pastor

L. O. Ramsey
Jackson Furniture

Marion Rightmer
Wilson Motor Co.

Edgar Vaught
Henna Motor Co.

Miss Lorraine Voigt
Wilson Motor Co.

O. A. Voigt
Tinner & Plumber

W. J. Walsh
R.R. White Lime Co.

F. R. Wilson
Wilson Motor Co.

O. R. Wilson
Stockbridge Gro.

Sam Bass Cafe

"Tiny" Bradley   Allen Bradley   "Porky" Bradley

Crimm Grocery & Market

H. N. Crimm   T. W. Burleson   Bill Kavanaugh

18

282

J.A. Nelson & Co.
Hardware - Implements - Lumber

PAINT UP
SHERWIN-WILLIAMS PAINTS

W. E. Henna   Floyd Carlson   Chas. Brotherman

E.R. Anderson Dairy

Which will extend the small private plant now in operation to the entire population within a year.

Only twenty miles away, construction on the great Marshall Ford Dam on the Colorado River is going forward at a rapid rate, insuring the citizens of this city and of this section of Texas a place for healthful recreation. Round Rock is well located near Central Texas' new system of lakes.

In looking toward a future that
(Turn to page 26)

Plant and crew of the Round Rock Cheese Co.

20

Lone Star Bakery

R. R. Moehring, Prop.

Brushy Creek showing one of its
three dams, with view of lake formed
by this dam.

21

Sexton Service Station
Sinclair Oil & Gas
On highways 2 & 81

Johnson Feed Store
Ernest A. Johnson, Prop.

It is only 8 miles from Round Rock to Southwestern University at Georgetown.

and only 18 to Texas Univ at Austin.

Live in Round Rock where it costs less and give your children a college education.

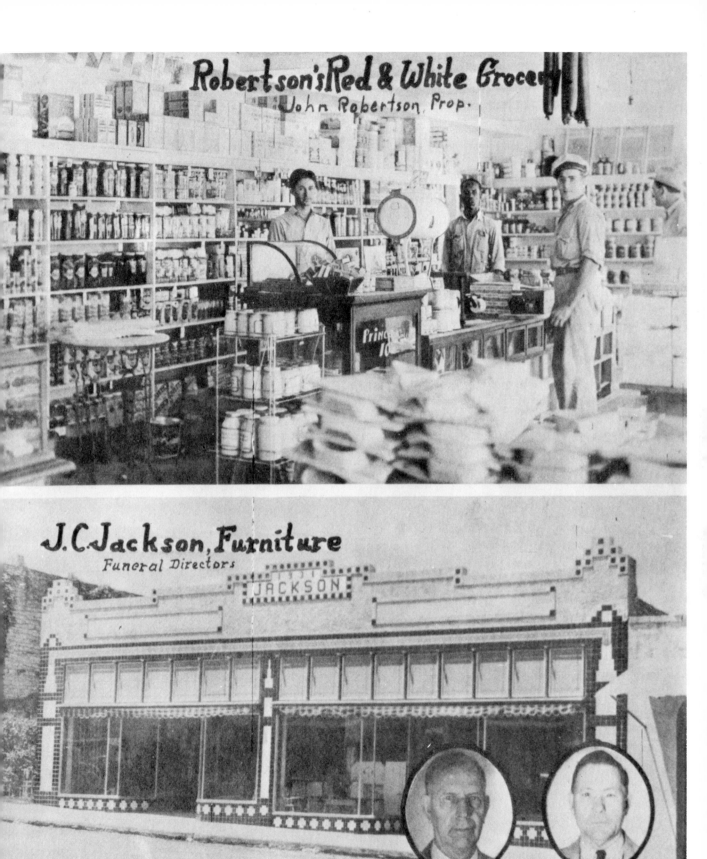

Robertson's Red & White Grocery
John Robertson, Prop.

J.C. Jackson, Furniture
Funeral Directors

JACKSON

J.C. Jackson   L.O. Ramsey

23

Texas Power & Light Co. Office

For eleven years the T. P. & L. has rendered faithful service to the people of Round Rock.....

Cody Adolphson
Local Manager

Mrs. Moody Mayfield
Bookkeeper

Lee "Butler" Bradley
Lineman

24

Street Scene on a normal day in Round Rock

Ethel's Beauty Shop

McNeese Gro.
Bess McNeese, Prop.

Baby Ruth

Linder's Shoe Shop
E. Linder, Prop.

Mayfield Service Station
Dick Mayfield, Prop.
Gulf Gas & Oil

Anderson Broom and
Mop Company.

has bright prospects, those whose efforts have made this progress possible should not be forgotten. The first city council was composed of men who worked earnestly to bring about the incorporation of the town. They were: John A. Nelson, Dr. W. G. Weber, E. J. Walsh, J. C. Jackson, W. A. Gantt, and A. K. Anderson.

Jack Jordon, the first mayor, has been city secretary since 1914. The other mayors during these 25 years:

(Turn now to page 32)

Farmers State Bank

Member Federal Deposit Insurance Corporation

T.E. Nelson
President

J.C. Jackson
Vice-President

G.R. Lundelius
Cashier

Leon Anderson
Asst. Cashier

Virgil Anderson
Bookkeeper

27

Public Service Garage

Bob Roberts
Proprietor

City Barber Shop
Martin Anderson, Prop.

Jackson Service Station
A.C. Jackson, Prop.
Texaco Products

28

Williamson County Old Settlers Association

Organized in 1904 at Georgetown

F. L. Aten
President

F. C. Humphreys, V. P. and Mgr.   Dr. T. M. Harrell Vice-Pres.

O.S.A. met first in Round Rock in 1923. Harrell Memorial Park is now permanent home of the Ass'n.   W. E. Henna, Treas.   Mrs. S. T. Atkin, Sec'y.

Headquarters cabin was moved from near Liberty Hill to its present location in 1936; was built in 1851.

O.S.A. Headquarters.

29

Dr. D.B. Gregg home

F.R. Wilson home

James Carlson home

John Jordon home

W.J. Walsh home

Gordon Noble home now under construction.

High Above THE REACH OF TREACHEROUS BRAZOS RIVER FLOOD WATERS SPEEDS GAS TO ROUND ROCK

When Brazos River reached record flood stage of 41 feet in 1936 bridge suspending 16-inch pipeline carrying natural gas south to Round Rock went out. Immediately Community Gas men went into action to build this new and stronger bridge within a few months. Now natural gas bound for Round Rock is safe from future Brazos flood waters in a huge pipeline suspended 20 feet above 1936 flood level. This is just part of a gas man's work to make certain the dependability of Round Rock's gas supply for its comfort and progress these next 25 years.

Community ★ Natural Gas Co.
LONE STAR GAS SYSTEM

We, the people of Round Rock are proud of the progress that has been made here in the past 25 years. Come to Round Rock to live and help us make still greater progress in the next 25 years.

The City of Round Rock, Texas.

Round Rock Has a Pure Water Supply

31

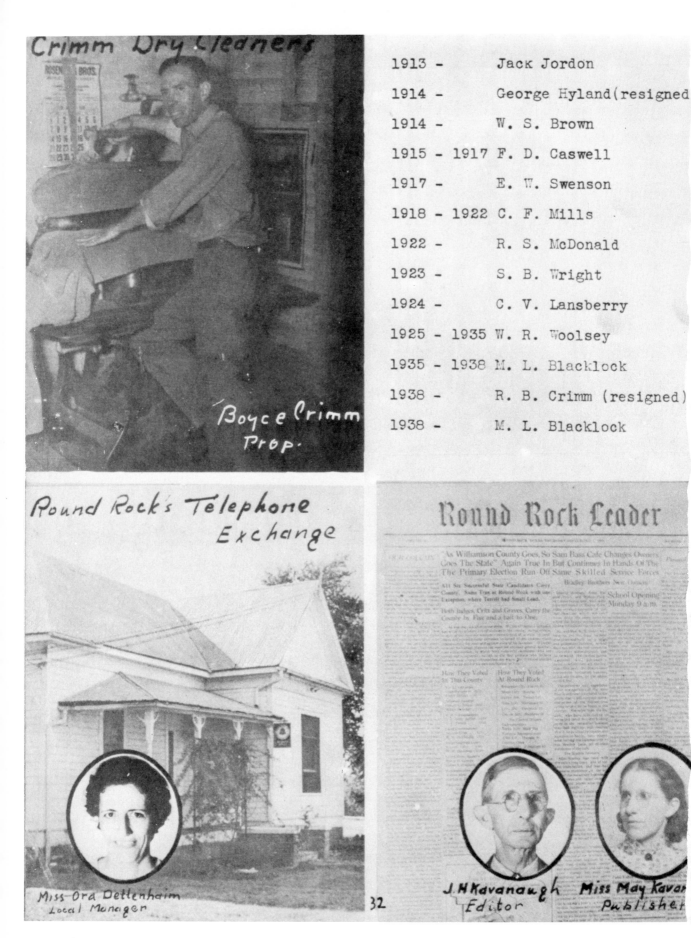

Crimm Dry Cleaners

Boyce Crimm
Prop.

1913 -		Jack Jordon
1914 -		George Hyland (resigned
1914 -		W. S. Brown
1915 -	1917	F. D. Caswell
1917 -		E. W. Swenson
1918 -	1922	C. F. Mills
1922 -		R. S. McDonald
1923 -		S. B. Wright
1924 -		C. V. Lansberry
1925 -	1935	W. R. Woolsey
1935 -	1938	M. L. Blacklock
1938 -		R. B. Crimm (resigned)
1938 -		M. L. Blacklock

Round Rock's Telephone Exchange

Miss Ora Dettenhaim
Local Manager

Round Rock Leader

"As Williamson County Goes, So Goes The State" Again True In The Primary Election Run-Off

Sam Bass Cafe Changes Owners But Continues In Hands Of The Same Skilled Service Forces

J. H. Kavanaugh
Editor

Miss May Kavan
Publisher

32